THE TRAGEDY OF THE HOGUE TWINS

HARRY OTTY

THE TRAGEDY OF THE HOGUE TWINS

To the Hogue family

'The Comeback Road'

So, we leave this game

which was hard and cruel,

and down at the show on a ringside stool,

we watch the next man

—just one more fool.

RANDOLPH (RANDY) TURPIN

World Middleweight Champion, 1951

CONTENTS

Jacumba, California, 1945
D & B Cafe on the right
(Photo courtesy of Cherry Diefenback - Jacumba Historical Society)

Advertisement for the D&B Cafe
(San Diego Union - June 13, 1937)

CHAPTER ONE

He was a sight to see, endowed with the ideal physique for a pugilist. Roughly 5 feet 8 inches tall and 160 pounds when in fighting trim. His beautifully muscled body, legs, and arms were the ultimate in physical perfection and, while he was a tad short for a middleweight, the distribution of mass gave him the ideal proportions for a fighter. His thick neck, heavy jaw and high cheekbones completed the perfect fighting face. The bright red cowboy boots and red Mackinaw, topped off with a Hollywood smile and a Stetson hat, completed the image of the sixth-ranked middleweight in the world.

At Potts' gym in Minneapolis, on the corner of 7th Street and Hennepin Avenue, Willis 'Shorty' Hogue, fighting pride of Jacumba, California, had left the temperate caress of his native state for the mid-winter grip of Minnesota. He was here to train for his January 9th fight with the No. 3 ranked welterweight in the world – Charley Burley of Pittsburgh. Having made his home in the Twin Cities, Burley had finished his one o'clock workout, but the gym chatter still hummed from the excitement his Saturday afternoon session had caused. Charley had gone 10 rounds with seven different sparring partners, each of whom could attest to how slick, clever and extremely heavy-handed he was.

George A. Barton, stalwart reporter for the *Minneapolis Tribune*, was on hand. Having interviewed Burley, he made a bee-line for Shorty and his manager, Tom Jones. To Barton, the pair must have looked like grandfather and grandson: Shorty, the young, smiling cowboy; and Jones, the wizened veteran who looked as if each and every trouble and heartache of his life had carved their marks upon his craggy features.

Hogue, who had turned 21 less than a week before, was a fast-rising force in the Californian boxing scene, and while everyone in Minneapolis was high on Burley, Shorty was not in town to make up the numbers. With a possible March meeting with middleweight champion of the world Tony Zale at stake, Shorty Hogue was here to win. Jones, at 68, was the oldest active manager in boxing. He had begun his career in 1896 serving as a matchmaker for the Eagles Lodge of La Salle, Ill., where he ran a saloon. It was there he discovered Billy Papke the *'Illinois Thunderbolt'* and guided him to the middleweight championship of the world in 1909. Jones steered Papke through 100 fights, four of them against the *'Michigan Assassin'* himself, Stanley Ketchel. By 1919 Papke was done as a fighter and by 1936 he was depressed and suspicious. So much so, that he shot his ex-wife dead before turning the gun on himself.

Tom's next world champion — Ad Wolgast — fared little better than Papke. King of the lightweights from 1910 to 1912 Wolgast was finished as a fighter by 1920. At age 50 he was living in a twilight world on the Californian farm of promoter Jack Doyle — convinced he would get another shot at Benny Leonard. For years Doyle had promised him a title shot with Leonard *'tomorrow,'* but for Wolgast tomorrow never came.

—A portent of things to come perhaps.

Less than two years previously, Jones had been a sick man, his soul ravaged by the cruel beasts that inhabit the world of boxing and life in general. When Shorty Hogue and his identical twin brother Big Boy (a welterweight) came along, Jones pepped up considerably and rediscovered his love for the game. "I've been managing fighters since 1896 and never handled anything but the best," said Jones. "I think I have the next middleweight champion in Hogue, if Uncle Sam doesn't order him to fight with a gun instead of gloves."

"What about Burley?" asked Barton.

"Boxing followers in Minneapolis and St. Paul, who know their fighters, will agree with me that Hogue is of championship caliber after he whips Burley. If I didn't think Hogue had the right stuff in him I wouldn't match him with Burley, who is the best welterweight in the game today."

There was little denying Burley's pedigree. He had come up the hard way in his native Pittsburgh, having been thrown to the wolves whilst still a mere cub in the professional fight game. Names such as Fritzie Zivic, Cocoa Kid, Jimmy Leto and Billy Soose littered his record; he had battled and beaten them all. Such was his superiority over Fritzie Zivic that the former welterweight champion of the world had bought out his contract to avoid having to fight him a fourth time.

With no willing opposition in the welterweight division, Burley had taken to accepting catch-weight fights with anyone willing to share the ring with him. Since arriving in Minneapolis with his wife and young daughter at the tail-end of 1941, he had fought twice, giving away 15 pounds to Ted Morrisson at the Minneapolis Armory on December 12 and spotting Jerry Hayes five pounds in a scheduled 10-rounder for a Christmas fund-raiser on the 23rd. Both fights ended in kayos for Burley and neither went more than four rounds.

By January of 1942, Burley had fought almost 50 times. He'd lost only five decisions and only one of his previous eight opponents had managed to hear the final bell. With the backing of local promoter Tommy O'Loughlin and manager Bobby Eaton, Charley was looking to tempt welterweight champion Freddie 'Red' Cochrane into a title fight in Minneapolis. Burley, when interviewed for *the Minneapolis Star Times* said, "I won't charge a penny to fight Cochrane in a fight for the benefit of the Red Cross, and I am sure Red, who is in the navy, would like to do his part."

Not to be outdone by Burley's bold rhetoric, Tom Jones told George Barton that Shorty Hogue was an 'old school' fighter. "Hogue can really fight," the veteran manager boasted, "If he couldn't, I wouldn't bother with him. He's willing to fight any opponent, including Burley, on a winner-loser basis." As it stood, Hogue had been guaranteed $1,300 by O'Loughlin and Burley significantly less. So a winner-loser purse of either 65-35 or 75-25, or even a 'winner-take-all' (possibly with a healthy side bet) would have been more to the Pittsburgher's liking.

"I have never fought anyone I didn't beat, so I can't see how things are going to change now," said Shorty. "I have met all these negro fighters everyone has stayed away from, and I won every time. I like these opponents everyone else is running away from." As Hogue implied, plenty of people had been running away from Charley Burley. Before securing Shorty's services, O'Loughlin (who claimed he had bought Burley's contract from Fritzie Zivic for $500) had originally matched his charge with Charley Parham for a fight at the Minneapolis Armory, but that fell though. Among the rated fighters Tommy contacted to step in as a replacement were Fritzie Zivic (by then a former champion), Mike Kaplan, Holman Williams, Izzy Jannazzo, Sammy Secreet, Young Kid McCoy, Ceferino Garcia, Coley Welch, Steve Belloise, Antonio Fernandez and Fred Apostoli; but there were no takers. Signing Shorty Hogue — the reigning California state middleweight champion — for a fight in Minneapolis was something of a coup for O'Loughlin, although it had come at a price; he knew he would be lucky to make his money back come fight night.

The *Minneapolis Star*'s Joe Hendrickson wrote that Charley was the favourite going into the fight, but only in terms of boxing ability. Some writers commented that Burley should have been called 'Surly'. He didn't like to speak to the press too much, didn't blow his own trumpet and was more than a little pissed off with the treatment he had received while climbing the rankings. Burley's only reply to the potential 12-pound weight difference was "I don't care what they weigh — just get me the fights and I'll prove I deserve a title chance in any division." His adversary for their battle at the Minneapolis Armory was his opposite — chatty, smiling, accommodating. Shorty made friends and fans from the minute his bright red cowboy boots hit the Minneapolis snow.

The Minneapolis Armory is a cavernous, sand-colored Art Deco building located at 500 South 6th Street. Constructed for the Minnesota National Guard it was completed in 1936 and was the costliest single building supported by a Public Works Administration grant. No stranger to boxing, having hosted numerous professional and local Golden Gloves events, it was a huge task for any promoter (or 'name' fighter) to fill it to its 10,000-seat capacity.

The action at the Armory started at 8:30 p.m. and, prior to the main event, those in attendance were entertained by preliminary bouts featuring John Flaherty vs Al Irwin, Jimmy Collins vs Ted Morrison, Wally Holm vs Carl Ford and Don Esperson vs Johnny Rozina.

Some 1,200 miles away in New York, the world heavyweight champion, Joe Louis, was defending his title for the 10th time as he went up against Buddy Baer. That event was to be relayed over the P.A. Fortunately for Tommy O'Loughlin and the paying fans, the Burley vs Hogue battle lasted a good deal longer than Louis' first-round demolition of Buddy Baer.

By 10.30p.m, the fans were ready for the main event:

A clash of styles which appears to favour Charley Burley, but not with enough certainty to cause Shorty Hogue to lose any sleep, makes the Jan 9 fistic battle at the Minneapolis Armory one of considerable debate.

Burley, the veteran campaigner, is a smooth boxer. He's smart, a nice jabber and a hard puncher. He's hard to hit. He rides the opposition punches and gets in his own through careful boxing. In other words, he is a ring master. Potts' gym observers can't remember a fighter who has shown more class here.

Hogue is the extreme opposite. Shorter than Burley, but 10 to 12 pounds heavier, the handsome, young San Diego middleweight is the type of fighter who constantly forces the action.

Keeping his head down, more-or-less buried in his bulging shoulders, Hogue tosses hook after hook with either hand and he never seems to stop.

Burley says he will out-box Hogue and jab out a decision by keeping his shorter, but heavier foe off balance, by making him miss. But there is a chance that Burley, who has not been too active because he has been tabooed by the good men, may run out of gas if the busy Hogue can force the fighting long enough. It must also be remembered that Burley's lighter weight advantage may hurry his tiring.

Everything adds up to a battle between two capable fighters with their own styles.

—Dick Cullum, *The Minneapolis Daily Times*

The boys' weights were announced as 163-1/2 for Shorty and 155 for Burley. The lighter man had actually weighed in at dead on 150 when he had his final workout on Thursday the 8th.

Referee Britt Gorman delivered the pre-fight formalities at ring centre before sending both combatants to their respective corners to await the first bell.

(Top) the twins with their mother, Pearl and (bottom) with their sister, Jessie (on the left) and their mother, Pearl (on the right).

(Photos courtesy of Bob and Lori Dye)

CHAPTER TWO

The spa town of Jacumba (*ha-koom-ba*) sits in a valley amongst the Jacumba Mountains 2,800 feet above sea-level. It is situated on the border with Mexico, less than half a mile from the small settlement of La Rumerosa. San Diego is around 75 miles to the west, and El Centro is 50 miles to the east. Prior to European occupation, the Kumeyaay peoples occupied Jacumba and surrounding areas. The warm, therapeutic springs were an attraction even then. Besides the native population, European ranchers discovered and occupied the area in the nineteenth century. There was frequent conflict with the local 'Indians' - none more famous than the February 27, 1880 Jacumba Massacre when around 15 natives were slain by ranchers who had accused them of cattle-rustling.

As the town grew, increasing numbers were being drawn to the hot spas, and by 1919, a rail link was developed with San Diego. Just five years later the town could boast the world class Hotel Jacumba, and a booming population. In the 1930s, the small mountain town had developed into a top destination and had a population of more than

500. Besides the railway, the town also had a bus station next to the famous Barbara Worth Cafe. The biggest attraction for Alonzo 'Lon' Hogue - most recently of Skiatook, Oklahoma - was the climate; particularly warm and dry with an average annual rainfall of less than 12 inches — ideal for a sickly asthmatic. Lon and his wife Pearl, a descendent of the Chickasaw tribe of Mississippi, were also drawn to the Imperial Valley area of California, a location that had recently attracted most of their family.

Of their eight children, five were old enough to work or have families of their own. While Simon, B. H. (Aka Duge), Nip, Jewell and Jessie got on with their lives, the youngest children - Betty and the twins Willis and Willard - still required the care and affection of parents. Simon, the eldest of the Hogue boys, had moved to Holtville to run a dairy farm and drive a truck. By the time he married his pregnant girlfriend, Mary Dell Bowman, in July 1924, other family members had begun to make the same trip out west.

Jacumba had an elementary school for the twins and plenty of cafés and hotels in which to find work. The town was so fine that Clark Gable frequented it during the boom years. Only 20 miles from Holtville and practically sitting in the middle of El Centro and San Diego, if one was looking to improve one's health or one's lot in life there were certainly worse places to be.

The Jacumba Hotel on State Highway 80 had some history — movie stars, singers, entertainers and politicians all took in its splendor. It was a true oasis in the desert. Pearl Hogue found herself a job in the kitchens there, but Lon was too weak to work full time. He had no energy for his young boys, and Betty was being brought up by Jessie Hogue and her husband Bob Plummer. They also had a son of their own – Richard, who was six years younger than Betty and eight years younger than the twins.

Lon and Pearl soon found the boys to be a drain, both on their energy and on their finances. A local couple - friends of the Hogue family - without children of their own offered to take the twins in, so they were fostered out to Glenn Briggs and his wife Grace.

Glenn Clark Briggs (known to just about everyone as Jim) was born in Nebraska in 1896. His WWI draft card from Knox, Nebraska, listed him as a 'Blacksmith-Horse Shoer,' — he was also a rodeo star in Imperial Valley and had successfully competed in a number of events with his buddy, Simon Hogue — but his trade on the 1930 census for Jacumba was 'Restaurant Owner.' His wife, known to all as 'Goldie' was six years younger. They were the perfect mix of experience, age and prosperity for parenthood. Running a cafe was hard and time-consuming work, but they somehow found the energy to contend with two hyperactive boys.

Although no one seems to know the exact reasons as to how the twins were given their distinctive nicknames, it appears that they were originally assigned them due to their stature and/or temperament. Willard was called 'Big Boy' because he was the bigger while Willis was dubbed 'Shorty' because he wasn't. It also seems that Big Boy never cried — ever — so he was 'Momma's Big Boy'. Shorty on the other hand, was very sensitive as a small child and cried a great deal. As the boys grew, Glenn and Goldie Briggs tended to the needs of the twins and their business while Pearl Hogue worked in the kitchen of the Jacumba Hotel and Lon hid himself away up in the hills where the air was more to his liking.

The twins attended Jacumba Elementary and entertained themselves on the corralled patch of land the Briggs' owned close to their business — the D & B Café — on Highway 80. Life was pretty idyllic for two young, energetic, horse-loving boys, but before they were even in their teens everything changed, and their childhood was snatched away. It may not have been evident at the time, but when their mother died on November 12, 1932, — just weeks before the twins' twelfth birthday — a fuse was lit; it was short and fast-burning.

The twins were doted on even more by Goldie Briggs, but no woman, no matter how hard she tries, can replace a boy's mother. Willard and Willis began fighting even more than usual; first with each other and eventually with anyone who looked sideways at them. Numerous family stories recount how they used to look for trouble and how they usually found it.

Jim Briggs knew a local service-station attendant named George Turner who had a reputation as a boxer. He approached him about training and coaching the boys in order to direct their energy, give them discipline and, and furnish a legitimate outlet for their new-found hatred of the world. Turner tried his best. He schooled the boys pretty well, but found it difficult to curb their enthusiasm for inflicting a beating on each other. If they were going to box, they would have to learn from each other; at least until they were schooled enough in the noble art to be matched against others in the region. In the meantime, they trained, they sparred, and they pummeled each other.

Their favorite battleground was the plot across from the D&B Café, and the locals knew them well and accepted what they were doing, even if the boys did occasionally overdo it. Anyone traveling through to the Coast, maybe stopping off for a coffee and something to eat, would have been shocked at the ferocity of the two young mountain lions going at each other. Sufficient numbers of locals and travelers were entertained to such a degree that the boys collected enough cash to view their scrapping as a business enterprise. Sometimes their enthusiasm would get the better of them.

The twins' nephew, Bob Dye (son of Wesley Dye and Jewell Hogue), remembered that the twins fought each other just about every day. He also recalls a time when the boys went a little too far:

"Boy, when they fought it was bad. People tried to stop them, but could not. Their dad was in Briggs' café, so my brother (Ben) went and got him. He came out and took a board off a fence and broke it on them trying to get them to stop — which they did; both bleeding."

—Bob Dye

Jim and Goldie bought the twins two beautiful brown and white pinto ponies, which they rode everywhere. Bob Dye recalls that his brother Ben rode behind Big Boy while he rode in back of Shorty. He remembers one particular adventure that occurred when they were riding close to the Mexican border - less than half a mile from Jacumba - and the boys spotted a bull on the other side of the fence. The twins crawled under the fence (and into Mexico) and approached the bull. When they got close, the bull charged and the twins took off like a couple of rockets. *"I did not know the twins could run so fast,"* Bob said. "When they got to the fence, they both slid under it, and that fence was low. I think all of us got a big laugh out of it."

Having brothers in the farming and rodeo business meant the twins also learned real cowboy skills to go along with their pugilistic prowess. Simon, Nip and Duge were a few years older than the twins (15, 14 and eight years respectively). Simon was always good to them and would, in later years, face some difficult decisions regarding their well-being. Simon was a solid family man who ran cattle and horses on his ranch in Holtville. Duge was a similar character, very strong and powerful, but with a heightened sense of fun; though on one occasion his goofing around backfired slightly. The boys were all eating dinner and Duge told the twins how, with no warning, he would sometimes without apparent reason just go crazy. Next thing, he just gets to twitching and jerking and freaking out. Shorty became frightened and stabbed Duge in the hand with a fork. By all accounts the stabbing was pretty bad as there was a lot of blood. Shorty took off running, but Duge couldn't help but laugh as he had caused the whole thing himself. Bob Dye said Duge, who earned his living as a fruit packer, just about had it all:

"Duge could whip both of the twins, one right after the other. He was about 5'-10", 160 pounds and looked like Tarzan.

One time I was with him at a carnival and the guy was calling for people to come over and wrestle - well, to make things short, Duge pinned one guy and slammed another. The second guy weighed about 220 pounds and could not believe Duge was so light.

When he took his wife to dance he would tap dance all around her, and one other thing - he could sing as good as Eddy Arnold. He missed the boat, had everything and did nothing with it."

—Bob Dye

The twins also had a musical bent, enjoying singing and playing guitar, but did not appear to have the talent their older brother possessed. Bob Dye said, "Their singing was not too good and neither was their playing — Duge was the entertainer of the family." Nip Hogue was the real black sheep of the family. He was a crack rodeo rider and a tough competitor, but he had a sinister side. He was a professional card player (and cheat) and later was involved in a good amount of criminal activity, especially when he relocated to the den of iniquity that was Reno, Nevada.

The twins would often ride up into the mountains to visit their dad who was becoming increasingly hermit-like. For one such visit, Big Boy thought he would go alone. His horse lost its footing on the rocky path, falling onto Big Boy, breaking his leg and injuring his hip. When he didn't return, Shorty, Richard Plummer, Bob Dye (the twins' nephews) and other family members went looking for him. They followed the usual path up, but it was starting to get dark, and there was still no sign of Big Boy. Fortunately, they heard him crying out just as they were about to turn around and head back to town.

By the time they were 14 and old enough to engage in local competitions, the twins had more rounds under their belts than just about any amateur boxer on the West Coast. El Centro and Brawley were the nearest locations for regular boxing events, and by the time they were ready for official fisticuffs their aggression appeared to intensify.

Besides boxing, both boys excelled at other sports. Shorty played running back and was a mainstay of the Mountain Empire football team. His bravery and tough nature was featured in a story in the local press, where it was reported that he severely injured his shoulder early in the first quarter of a game against the older and heavier El Centro B squad. Despite the handicap and an inability to carry the ball effectively, Shorty played on as a blocking-back. At the final whistle the referee was quoted in the local press as saying, "There, by gad, is the gamest, grittiest kid I've seen on a football field." As his boxing career took off, such qualities would be both a blessing and a curse.

Willard (Big Boy) and Willis (Shorty) Hogue.
(Photo courtesy of Bob and Lori Dye)

ROUND 1

Minneapolis: Friday January 9, 1942

"If Hogue can trap Burley and administer his rapid-fire punishment before Burley can resume his nifty footwork, Burley may suffer."

—Joe Hendrickson, *Minneapolis Star Times*

CHAPTER THREE

On May 24, 1936, while he was out with the boys at a rodeo in Imperial Valley, Lon Hogue sat under a tree, closed his eyes and never opened them again. His youngest boys were only 15 and were just finding their way in the local boxing scene.

Lon died just two days prior to the boys' planned bouts at the Brawley Athletic Club. Shorty was distraught and couldn't compete. Big Boy was also devastated, but decided to go ahead anyway. His opponent, Pete Lugo of the host club, probably wished that Big Boy had followed his brother's lead:

> "Willard Hogue, Jacumba battler, stole the show however, with the best exhibition of fighting seen in the Brawley ring this year.
>
> He started inauspiciously enough against Pete Lugo, coolly feeling out the Brawley fighter. Lugo tried to reach the Jacumba boy with a fast right but Hogue rolled away from the

punch and retaliated with a straight, hard left that stunned Lugo.

Hogue held Lugo off with a beautiful defensive and baffled Pete with a series of lefts and rights to the face, each blow taking its toll. In the second round, Hogue followed Lugo and suddenly slapped Pete to the floor with a left and right cross. Lugo got up at the count of eight only to return to the canvas for another eight-count.

Beginning the third, Lugo came out battered, but game. Mercilessly, Hogue pasted Lugo with rights and lefts and Lugo met the canvas three times before Tackett stepped in to stop the bout at 1 minute and 12 seconds of the third.

As Hogue left the ring, the fans leaped to their feet and wildly applauded the Jacumba fighter as the greatest amateur to show in the Brawley arena."

—The Brawley Press

Big Boy was described in the press as a "cherub faced, well-built 126 pounder." The same report stated that he looked like "a real prospect."

Just a week after their dad's funeral, both Hogue boys fought together on an amateur card in Imperial Valley. Shorty, probably still needing to unload his grief and anger, dealt a beating to Robert Harris, knocking him out in the final round of a scheduled four-rounder. Big Boy, his rage only slightly dissipated, beat Harry Arrington on points over the same distance. The Hogue twins were becoming increasingly popular in local boxing circles; in less than three years the whole boxing nation would be aware of them.

On June 9, 1936, George Turner matched them again for a show in El Centro. Shorty defeated Mayo Sario over four rounds, and Big

Boy repeated the trick against Joe Morrissett; the victories kept coming:

"HOGUE TWINS TAKE WINS IN BRAWLEY

Hitting Joe Gonzales at will, Willard Hogue Tuesday night pounded out a four round decision over the Calexican in the main event at the Brawley Eagles club.

Hogue demonstrated his abilities as a defensive fighter in the first round by keeping out of reach of Gonzales' wild swings. Ducking, dodging and rolling with the punches, Hogue suddenly unleashed an offensive in the second stanza that kept the game but outclassed Gonzales on the run throughout the rest of the battle.

Willis Hogue handed Cleo Shans a beating in the semi-wind-up. He slapped the negro all over the ring hitting him with both hands. If the negro landed a blow in the fight, no one saw it. Hogue started to work in the first canto and kept up his relentless attack until the final bell sounded."

—The Brawley Press, July 22, 1936

Although there is some evidence to suggest that the twins may have taken part in organized amateur bouts during the last few months of 1935, most newspapers indicate that their first recorded bouts were in the second quarter of 1936. One family record (listing most of their amateur bouts) sees them having their first bouts in May and June of that year. Additional research has so far determined that between May and December 1936 Shorty Hogue fought 21 times while Big Boy had 18 contests.

The following press reports are from a family scrapbook (kindly provided by Lori Dye). While many of the press cutting have dates, they do not always include the source. As most of the twin's early career was centred around Brawley, Holtville and El Centro, it is fairly safe to assume that the clippings came from the local papers; the most popular of which would be the *Imperial Valley Press* and the *Morning Post* (El Centro). The following is from the *Brawley Press* (July 29, 1936):

> "Frances Richards, the clowning boxer from San Bernardino, must have been "clowning" last night, for he did not show up at the Eagle Arena for the main event in which he was carded for a go with "Big Boy" Hogue of Jacumba. Consequently, it was necessary for Matchmaker Al Finkbeiner to enter a substitute. Dave Guererro was put in to 'pinch hit' for Richards.
>
> Hogue blasted him around the ring in the first round ,and before the end of the second, referee Bill Tackett awarded the fight to the mountain lad on a technical knockout.
>
> Willis "Shorty" Hogue, "Big Boy's" twin brother, kayoed Joe Murio in the semi-wind-up. He was given the decision in the second round."

In 1936, Big Boy went eight fights before his first setback, a points loss to Joe Garcia (whom he defeated in a rematch), but it would be much longer before Shorty would see his opponent's hand raised against him. Following the win over Joe Murio, Shorty stepped up to defeat sailors Fred Koch (*USS Dale*), Billy Potts (*USS Tennessee*), and Johnny Jarred (*USS Fox*). Big Boy, not to be outdone by his twin, also defeated Koch and Potts. Shorty stopped Potts in two rounds, while Big Boy was forced to go the distance. The only other significant difference was that Shorty was 15 years old at the time of his victories and Big Boy was 16 when he turned the trick in April 1937.

Also in April 1937, both boys faced off against Bill White of nearby Brawley. Big Boy on the 14th and Shorty on the 20th of the month:

"That Bill White is tough was definitely proved in the Brawley A.C. Arena Tuesday night when the San Bernardino whirlwind took a severe drubbing from the fists of Shorty Hogue, but refused to go down.

White, realizing he was in for a mighty tough bout, was cautious throughout the fight. He stopped back-peddling only two or three times, and then Shorty's blows would send him back to his bicycle.

The Hogue twin won every round and when it was all over fans still did not know which twin was the best. Big Boy whipped White in El Centro Thursday and Shorty was just as decisive last night.

Big Boy threw three terrific left hooks and a short left uppercut to stop Jimmy Lyons of San Diego in the second round of the semi-wind-up.

Lyons, who last year kayoed Gene Boatwright, and who this year was undefeated, sent in a flurry of blows in the first round to make the fight interesting. But just before the bell, Big Boy nipped the San Diegan with a sizzling left and Lyons dropped like a window weight. The bell saved him from a kayo.

When Lyons went down in the second round, however, he was down for keeps and his seconds carried him to his corner.

Art Gonzales of San Diego grabbed a decision over Everette Jure in the sixth battle. Gonzales was too tough and threw too many punches for the Ontario middleweight."

—*Brawley Press,* April 21, 1937

It was apparent that both boys were a little too good for any of the local competition. According to available records Shorty had scored

10 knockouts in his 21 bouts, while Big Boy had stopped six of his opponents inside the distance.

Just a week after their victories over White and Lyons, both boys were back in the ring in El Centro. Big Boy - already the San Diego Valley lightweight champion — was contesting the Imperial Valley lightweight title against 'Jolting' Joe Villegas. Big Boy was listed as 3-1/2 inches taller than the 5-foot-4-inch Villegas, but both had the same 69-inch reach. The most curious statistic reported in the local press was that of the protagonists ages; Villegas was listed as 20, while Big Boy was down as 18. The truth was that the taller man was in fact only 16 years old.

They started to get their picture in the local papers as public interest in them grew. On April 29, 1937, Big Boy was featured in an article about his upcoming title-bout tussle with Joe Villegas of El Centro:

"BIG BOY TO CLASH WITH JOLTER JOE

Jacumba's Hogue twins, two of Southern California's most outstanding lightweights, will risk their records in the El Centro A.C. ring Thursday night in the main event and semi-windup. Big Boy will clash with Jolting Joe Villegas in the main event. The winner will be declared the champion of San Diego and Imperial Counties.

Big Boy and Villegas have met the best among invading lightweights this season and have made every opponent seek cover before the final bell. Big Boy lost a questionable decision to Tommy Young, and Villegas defeated Young the following week."

—*El Centro Morning Post*, April 29, 1937

According to a number of local press reports, Shorty would have his work cut out for him in his fight on the same bill. He was matched with Don Benzor, a former Southern California lightweight champion. Benzor had not lost his title in the ring, but was no longer the reigning champ, having missed the entry deadline for the 1937 tournament. Described in the press as "a powerful puncher who has dropped few decisions over his extended career." - Benzor appeared a formidable opponent:

"Shorty Hogue meets an equally tough opponent in Don Benzor, former Southern California lightweight champion. Benzor defeated Jure last week and appears to be in even better condition than when he walloped the best boxers on the Coast last season.

He kayoed Boatwright, decisioned Villegas and whipped a list of the best in the valley last year in El Centro fights.

Shorty has never been defeated and will give the veteran Benzor a great battle. Shorty is hard to hit and packs dynamite in both fists.

Noel Johnson, El Centro matchmaker, has lined up an outstanding support card. Manuel Ortiz will meet Ray Martinez of Calexico in the fifth bout. Ortiz dropped a close fight to Martinez on a foul last season and has been looking forward to a return match ever since. Martinez will enjoy a slight weight advantage, but Ortiz is certain he can take the Calexican down the line.

Loudermilk and Adams will clash in a rematch. Loudermilk took the decision last week, but Adams' supporters claim the Brawley boy was robbed. Galloway and Ortega, who staged a slam bang battle last week, will also meet in a rematch."

—*El Centro Morning Post,* April 29, 1937

As had previously been the case, age and experience appeared no barrier for the twins:

"Imperial Valley turned out last night to see a champion crowned, and was not disappointed. Big Boy Hogue, Jacumba's package of dynamite, came through with flying colors to blast Jolting Joe Villegas from his valley lightweight throne and take for himself the San Diego and Imperial County championship.

Big Boy Hogue did not claim all the glory of the night however, for Shorty, his twin brother, slammed through four vicious rounds to take an impressive decision over Don Benzor, former Southern California lightweight champion, in the semi-windup.

Villegas suffered his most severe beating in two years of competition in losing to Big Boy, but he went down fighting. The first round was about even with Hogue taking a slight advantage in the infighting. The second and third cantos were tucked away in Big Boy's bag in a decisive manner. He just threw more punches.

Villegas, who has won a majority of his fights with telling blows in the clinches, was no match for the Hogue twin in infighting. Again and again, Big Boy jarred the former valley champion with short lefts and rights.

The fourth round was the fastest of the bout despite the fact both fighters were tired. Villegas desperately tried for a KO but could not land his vicious right. Hogue, however, continually sunk rights and left hooks that sent Villegas to his corner at the bell in a dazed condition.

SHORTY SHOWS WELL

Shorty, after a rather slow start wound up the fight in a blaze of fists and glory. The first round was close and a Post-Press score-sheet gave Benzor a slight edge. The second round was a nightmare for the Casa Blanca boy, however, for Shorty found the range with his left jab.

He jabbed Benzor until fans at ringside marveled at Benzor's stamina. A right cross at the bell nearly sent Benzor to the canvas.

He came out strong for the third, however, and held the Hogue twin even until the final half-minute of the stanza. In that half-minute Shorty dished out punishment that a less experienced fighter would not have survived.

The fourth round was fast and furious with Shorty again taking the edge. Benzor was bleeding at the mouth and nose as the final bell clanged simultaneously with one of Shorty's powerful jabs."

Future two-time bantamweight champion of the world, Manuel Ortiz, also impressed the crowd in his fight on the bill:

"ORTIZ GAINS REVENGE

Manuel Ortiz made Ray Martinez forget that he was ever a fighter in the fifth bout when the El Centro battler avenged a previous defeat at the hands of Martinez. Ortiz lost a decision to the Calexican on a foul last year.

The first round was slow with Manuel trying to get past Martinez's long arms. In the second, Ortiz opened up with a whirlwind attack that deposited Martinez on the floor twice. Martinez again hit the canvas in the third round and was down three times in the fourth before Tackett stopped the bout."

A booster of the twins was one J. G. Wirt of Calipatria, California. He wrote to Braven Dyer's 'Sports Parade' column in the *LA Times*:

"...the boys possess remarkable style and will outclass many professionals right now. Both have good lefts, hit with short punches rather than long swings, and carry knockout force in either hand. From the start, it has been necessary for local matchmakers to put them against boys over their weight to make interesting fights. 'Shorty' now weighs around 130, and 'Big Boy' around 135. Atop this, both boys are clean, good-looking youngsters who pack arenas with their admirers every time out."

According to a June 15, 1937 press report on Shorty's upcoming battle with Tony Deval, the eldest of the Hogue twins was unbeaten in 29 fights. Deval, fighting out of the Main Street Gym in LA, was described as "...an experienced amateur and rated one of the best prospects in the lightweight division." Deval's gym-mate - Johnny Castillo, who was to oppose Big Boy on the same card — was deemed to be as good, but appeared not to carry the same punch as Deval, who boasted a 50-percent KO record. In the battle of the big punchers, it was Shorty who came up with the kayo (round 4) for win number 30. Big Boy beat Castillo over the four round distance. Shorty's winning ways came to an end in his next bout against the experienced Ulysses *'Uley'* Harris of the LA Newsboys gym:

"An inch-and-a-half cut over Shorty Hogue's right eye tonight broke his sensational 31-fight-winning streak when Uley Harris, Los Angeles negro, was awarded a technical KO over the twin in the third round of the semi wind-up.

Uley Harris, rated the best lightweight in Los Angeles County, won the first round of his fight against Shorty, but was losing ground in the second round when his head bumped Shorty and made a gash in the twin's eye.

Referee Bill Tackett and George Barnett, handler of the twin, would not let Shorty continue the fight, although he protested vigorously against quitting."

—*The Imperial Times,* June 23, 1937

The same report said that Big Boy had pounded out a four-round win over Johnny Castillo, who was saved by the bell on two separate occasions. The Main Street Gym fighter was obviously not convinced Big Boy had beaten him a couple of weeks earlier. Shorty's chance to reverse the loss to Harris was not long in coming as at the end of July, he was again ready for action. This was his first bout back after allowing his cut to heal, but he appeared to have trained to the limit for this main event bout at the Brawley A.C. Arena:

"Harris came out of his corner fast in the opening round, but Shorty refused to allow the negro to get close enough to land his favorite left hook.

The fighters sparred for a moment in the center of the ring before Shorty cut loose with a barrage of rights and lefts that drove the Los Angeles battler across the ring.

Harris didn't have a show from the opening bell of the second round and absorbed a beating that a less capable battler would not have been able to stand up under.

The third round was a repetition of the first two, and Harris was hanging on at the bell. The Los Angeles negro begged his trainer to stop the fight between the third and fourth cantos, but (Frankie) Garcia refused to heed Harris' plea.

Harris refused to budge when the bell rang, but Garcia pushed him to the center of the ring to meet Shorty. Harris threatened to foul the twin as the fighters clinched unless Hogue would

29

take it easy, but Shorty clipped the negro with a right and a left as they broke.

The negro reeled momentarily, then clinched again and kneed Shorty three times before referee Bill Tackett could step in and stop the fight."

— *Imperial Times,* July 21, 1937

After Big Boy lost to Wilson Mackey and Cleo McNeil, both experienced fighters with a few years on him, the boys started what became a curious practice. If one Hogue lost to a fighter, then the second Hogue would attempt to gain revenge. Shorty challenged Mackey twice in quick succession, the second time (in August 1937) for the Lightweight Championship of California. The *Imperial Valley Press* reported:

"Shorty Hogue, Jacumba lightweight, who packs power in both fists, had to extend the limit of his power and endurance in the Brawley arena Tuesday night to pound out a close decision over Wilson Mackey in the main event.

The Los Angeles negro, who was the toughest fighter Shorty has encountered in the Brawley ring, threw leather with a skill that indicated plenty of experience. He held Shorty even in the first round, and then landed the most punches in the second to win the stanza.

In the third Shorty, who was bothered by the peculiar style the negro had in the first two rounds, began to work faster and more confidently to take a slight edge.

The fourth round however, was all Shorty. His superior hitting power and fine defensive tactics began to take their toll, and the negro absorbed a lacing in the final stanza to lose the fight."

The decision of the judges was split, but the fans were unanimous in their appreciation of both fighters. The only argument appeared to be between Shorty's nephews, Bob Dye (age 11) and Richard Plummer (10) who argued Shorty's championship status for almost 15 minutes. One insisted that their uncle was state champion, while the other argued that he wasn't state champion, but was the California champion. The dispute was settled by Bob's older brother, Ben, who told the boys that California was the state they were in, and Shorty was its champion.

Wilson Mackey would turn to the pro ranks in 1939. His career was interrupted in 1942 by the war. He served a stint in the Army, winning an Inter-Service title at middleweight after a six-day tournament in Algeria. Marcel Cerdan of France (future world middleweight champion) won a "senior welterweight" title, and Californian Larry Cicneros won at welterweight.

On September 16, 1937, Shorty defeated Joe Villegas by KO in the fourth round before dropping a close decision to Miller Fonseca. Shorty would have to wait until he was in the pro ranks before he was able to exact revenge on Fonseca. As it turned out, the twins' biggest opponent wouldn't be wearing boxing gloves, but would instead be wielding a pen. Persons unknown reported that there was an issue with the twins' age. They wouldn't turn 17 until the end of the year — yet here they were taking on and beating adults for open titles.

Considered too good to fight in the youth divisions and too young to compete with the men, both boys were stood down and had to survive with no official competition for almost 12 months. Both came back stronger than ever and would prove nigh-on impossible to beat. In the intervening year they played football at high school, but didn't apply themselves any more to their studies. They even managed to get involved in some rodeo action with their brother Nip and won prizes for roping and lassoing.

Their local fame meant there was no shortage of female admirers. Big Boy managed to rope himself a beauty in the form of Frances Sieber, a local dress store employee who had moved from New York to California with her parents and her two sisters. Frances was 2-1/2 years older than Big Boy, but that didn't prevent them getting married. Glenn Briggs as "step-father and guardian of Willard Joseph Hogue, a minor, of the age of 18 years" signed his consent on the affidavit for the marriage license, though he may have done so with his fingers crossed. The date of the affidavit is October 6, 1937. Big Boy would have been 16 at the time, Frances 19. It is possible Frances was already pregnant when they were married, as their first child, Jimmie Burton Hogue, was born in June, 1938. As a married man, Big Boy found a new home for his family at 144 A Street, Jacumba.

With a string of admirers of his own, it seemed inevitable that Shorty would be leaving the Briggs' nest at 209 US Highway 80 - the Main Street in Jacumba:

"Once when I was in Jacumba Shorty said *'Let's ride the horses to the park',* so he got his horse and I got Briggs' horse Tex. When we got to the park, we rode around. Shorty said he knew a girl that lived on a hill nearby. So we went up the hill, and the girl came out. It didn't take me long to get tired of that. Shorty said, *'Go on back, and I'll will be home before long.'*

Of course because of the girl, and Shorty was older, I would put on a show. I got the horse running down the hill. There was an old wash house and a road that no car had been on in years, oh yea there was a car this time and hit my horse in the side and me going fast as I can. I went over Tex's head, and he fell almost on top of me.

I broke my right arm and Tex had a cut on his side. Shorty came running down to see how bad things were. He picked me up and put me on the horse and I had to ride that horse with a broken arm. Boy that ride was not very smooth, but I got home. Tex was OK after they put car grease on his side. And me, 54 miles to a doctor!"

—Bob Dye

As the 1938 boxing season approached, the twins knew they would soon face a major decision. Both were still growing, and their return to boxing in September 1938 would coincide with the run-up to the senior championships. With a long-standing agreement not to oppose each other in the ring, it was obvious that one of them would have to move up a weight category when the time came for the championships.

For the fighter that moved up in weight, this would be an important, and possibly life-changing decision.

Mirror, mirror on the wall, who's the toughest of them all?
Shorty and Big Boy (photo courtesy of Mike Silver)

ROUND 2

Minneapolis: Friday January 9, 1942

"In the early stages Hogue's stubborn aggressiveness and his ability to take Burley's sharp shooting and wade in for shots at the body made the going close."

—Dick Cullum, *Minneapolis Daily Times*

"Get the picture, Hogue slowly advancing, throwing heavy roundhouse hooks as the faster Burley sniped with his jab and crossed with his right."

—Joe Hendrickson, *Minneapolis Star Times*

CHAPTER FOUR

In August and September 1938, the twins were back on the local boxing scene with a bang, Shorty with a second round kayo of Ivan Lewis and Big Boy with a four round points win over Vic Villavincencia. Both boys continued to cut a swathe through the local opposition until September 22, 1938, when Shorty appeared to have a lucky escape:

"Kent Roberts, welterweight champion of the Far West, suffered a 'home-town' decision loss at the El Centro Athletic Club Thursday night when Judges Roy Cantrell and Bonner Williams gave Shorty Hogue the verdict over the Los Angeles negro in the main event.

Roberts, a southpaw who eked out a decision over Art Gonzales of San Diego in the finals of the Golden Gloves tournament last year and then went on to win the Far West title by a knockout, rallied in the fourth round of his battle with Shorty Thursday to take an edge that should have netted him the win.

But the judges, giving Shorty an edge in two of the first three rounds, cast their ballots for the twin from Jacumba and it was all over but the booing. Shorty took the first round with a barrage of fists, and took the second by a narrow margin. Then Roberts began to find the range. He won the third by a slight margin and took the fourth in apparently easy fashion.

In the semi-windup, Big Boy Hogue, subbing for Herman Graves, pummelled Martin Vasquez mercilessly to take every round and a decision over the Los Angeles battler. Hogue, who was not prepared to fight until two weeks from Thursday, was not in the form that saw him kayo Clem Waske two weeks ago. His punches were not as sharp, but his defense was functioning well enough to ward off Vasquez blows."

—*Imperial Valley Press,* September 23, 1938

The boys found their true form soon enough as both Shorty and Big Boy went on to record four more wins before the end of October. With boxing, family, and school, both boys had a full calendar. In its annual election of officers (October 1938), the Mountain Empire High School listed Big Boy as Vice President of the junior students while Shorty was elected as 'Social Commissioner'.

On November 16 the twins were due to appear together at a local tournament, but Big Boy had to pull out due to a hip injury. The fans and the promoter were undoubtedly disappointed with not getting to see the usual double dose of Hogue mayhem, but Shorty had an idea; he would fight his opponent and Big Boy's opponent too. The local press ran the following:

"CALEXICO, *Nov. 16 (special)*—Shorty Hogue took the all-division amateur fight crown back to Jacumba with him tonight, and there was no challenger brave enough to raise their voice in protest.

There were no challengers because Shorty came out in the fourth bout to decisively trounce Ray Velarde, and returned in the final scrap to all but knock Frankie Jackson from the ring.

Velarde outweighed Shorty four pounds, and Jackson tipped the scales 12 pounds above Shorty's weight, but both may as well have been in the featherweight division for all the chance they had. Shorty's double duty was forced on him when his twin brother, Big Boy Hogue, suffered a hip injury Tuesday night in training.

Velarde didn't have a chance from the opening bell of Shorty's first battle. The twin peppered him with rights and lefts that brought blood and raised welts.

Velarde hit the ground for a five-count in the third round.

Jackson put up a slightly better battle than Velarde, but was unable to land solidly or consistently. Hogue on the other hand landed with both fists and had Jackson on the verge of slumber at the end of the third and fourth rounds.

Big Boy's hip injury, a recurrence of an old hurt, may be serious enough to force him out of the Golden Gloves tournament."

According to the local media, the fight with Jackson was Shorty's first foray into the middleweight ranks as he gave away 12 pounds in weight and a significant amount of reach.

With regard to the regional championships, the twins had to decide which of them would remain at their natural weight class of 147 pounds and who would move up to 160 pounds. According to Bob Dye, they decided that the twin with the better record against heavier fighters would compete at middleweight, while the other would stay in the welterweight division. This is supported by an article written by Jack James of the *Los Angeles Examiner* (December 1, 1938):

"So, in order to avoid the embarrassing eventuality of possibly having either to fight with or default to his twin, the boys decided that one of them would have to go in the welterweight division—the natural bracket—and the other in the middleweight.

Their method of deciding which was to make the sacrifice—though neither regarded it in that light—was unique. They determined that over a period of two months each should fight the same 160-pounders in the amateur ranks, the outcomes to settle the issue.

Willis (Shorty) won 'em all by knockouts in the first or second round. Willard (Big Boy) won 'em all too—but in the course of one engagement he got clipped and knocked off his feet, thereby spoiling the family fistic record. So Willard (Big Boy) resigned in favour of Willis (Shorty). And when it came time for the weigh-in Shorty went out and took on a load of fodder that brought his normal 146 pounds up into the lower brackets of the middleweight class."

According to the twins known records for 1938, there are no common opponents listed for the period prior to them entering the Golden Gloves. From September 2 to November 29 — when the preliminary rounds of the tournament got underway — Big Boy had 13 fights to Shorty's 14. While the one bout advantage appears to be the result of Shorty fighting twice on November 16, the real point of difference is in the kayo numbers — Shorty had seven inside the distance wins to Big Boy's four.

Another clue to how things may have been shaping up for the twins weight-wise is a small (undated) clipping found in a family scrap-book. A picture of Shorty with the title 'Middleweight' across the top states "Shorty Hogue, scheduled to fight Herman Graves for the championship of the Far West on Sept. 29." No report or result has been found for said bout — although that does not mean it didn't take place. What is known however, is that Herman Graves did not enter the Golden Gloves that year, but instead turned to the pro ranks, where he made his debut on November 8.

While it was a close call, what little evidence there was supported the conclusion that Shorty should be the one to move up. For one thing, while Big Boy had yet to step out of the welterweight class, Shorty had already defeated Frankie Jackson, a legitimate middleweight. For another, Shorty had beaten Wilson Mackey twice — their most recent common opponent — whereas Big Boy had lost a decision to him. And finally, Shorty was now slightly taller and boasted the better overall kayo percentage than Big Boy. In any event, and whatever the logic, it was Shorty who stepped up into the middleweight division for the upcoming championships.

Besides substituting for one another, the twins were able to profit from their remarkable physical likenesses. Whenever they fought on the same card, they would challenge their respective opponents to wager one dollar on whether they could guess which Hogue brother they had fought. According to Bob Dye, the twins never lost a single bet.

If their opponents had a little 'inside knowledge' about the twins they may have had better luck in the betting game. Unknown to them, Big Boy had a scar on his forearm where a coyote bit him. It seems that Big Boy had captured the animal and, thinking he could domesticate it, tied it up in the yard like a dog. Apparently, the coyote didn't take to kindly to its confinement and went after Big Boy the first chance it got.

As the end of November approached, both boys were unbeaten for the year and were looking forward to continued success in the *LA Examiner* Golden Gloves. As a national tournament, the annual event was popular, and entries for the LA region alone were massive. With a staggering 230 boxers featured in the original draw, there were 47 entries in the welterweight class and 36 entries in the middleweight division. Just two weeks after Shorty's doubleheader against Jackson and Velarde, Big Boy took a four-round decision from Jack Thompson in the preliminary rounds of the 1938 Golden Gloves in Los Angeles. Some 8,000 fans, and a number of Hollywood film celebrities, enjoyed the action.

Shorty and Big Boy came through the second set of preliminary rounds later in November with victories over William Gugler and Bob Cramer, respectively. The last 16 in each division then lined up against each other at the Olympic Auditorium on December 1. Shorty had few problems defeating Colbert Broussard of Bakersfield, whilst Big Boy received a walkover as Roy Harrison (unattached) defaulted on their bout.

Local sportswriter, Bill Potts, reported on the pulsating quarter-final stages:

> "Twenty-four bouts are on schedule with the boys making biff-steak out of each other in sixteen semi-final and 8 final round classics.
>
> The starting gate goes up promptly at 8 o'clock with only one ring in operation. Couldn't use the other one if they wanted to, Willis (Shorty) Hogue and Johnny Wilkes all but tore it down and beat each other over the head with the debris in the last bout Thursday night.
>
> *Shorty's* ears are still ringing today from one of the greatest ovations ever given an amateur boxer here.
>
> Knocked down twice by Wilkes, probably the smoothest boxer and hardest hitter in the middleweight division, 'Shorty' bounced off the floor like a golf ball and after a dozen toe-to-toe exchanges, in which he caught everything but the first ball

pitched in the 1938 World Series, the raging Hogue finally made Wilkes break ground.

Once *Shorty* made his man break ground, he started making him cover it—full speed backwards. Cornering Wilkes just before the final bell, Hogue let loose with such an unmerciful barrage of leather he unanimously won what otherwise would have been anyone's fight."

Local reporter Burdette Kinne of the *El Centro Post Press* also described the frenetic action witnessed in Shorty's smashing, crashing victory over Wilkes:

"Shorty's test came in the Southern California eliminations, Big Boy's in the final bout of the far western tournament.

Guy Wilkes, a negro middleweight, proved Shorty's toughest opponent in the entire tournament. Wilkes smashed Shorty to the canvas with a right to the chin in the third round of a quarter-final bout in the Southern California eliminations.

But Shorty bounced back to his feet to hand Wilkes the worst beating of his career. Shorty threw caution to the winds, waded in with both fists flying. Wilkes did the only sensible thing; he backed up. If he hadn't Shorty's flailing fists would have sent him into slumberland."

The *LA Times* called the Hogue-Wilkes contest, "One of the greatest amateur ring battles in local history." Shorty had to do it all over again on December 5th when he tangled with Jimmie Coleman (unattached), while Big Boy fought Cecil Hudson (unattached). Both boys came through those battles to set up final showdowns with Sammy Nero and Art Gonzales.

Again, Bill Potts for the local press, covered the action:

"Willard, or Big Boy, the welterweight, turned in a finished performance to completely dominate his fight with Art Gonzales, a Mexican boy who has been nothing but poison all through the tournament. Willard made the decision more emphatic by flooring the scrappy Gonzales for a no-count in the third round.

Willis 'Shorty' Hogue followed his happy brother into the battle pit and neatly disposed of a socking sailor in the person of Sammy Nero of the U.S.S. Holland.

Appropriately enough, Shorty also scored a no-count knockdown, with Nero hitting the floor under the impact of a terrific right hand in the first round. Although Shorty's victory was without question, he apologized for his showing by revealing that he was suffering from an attack of the flu, with which he was stricken when he drove to his home near San Diego after Thursday night's show."

After adding senior state titles to the ones they had won as youth boxers, both boys were now on to the Tri-State box-offs to determine the West Coast entries into the national finals in Detroit the following January. The local press, in a piece promoting the Tristate Finals, ran a photograph of both boys and a set of scales:

"WEIGHTY PROBLEM—In answer the oft-repeated question 'What do those Hogue twins actually weigh?' The scrappy brothers stepped on the scales for the cameraman last week. Fully clothed, Willard, the welterweight, tipped 148 and Willis, the middleweight, 153.

Allowing five pounds for the clothes would bring their respective weights to 143 and 148, meaning they must spot their foes five to 12 pounds in every bout. They will try to overcome the handicap again when they face classy boys from

44

Seattle and San Francisco tonight at the Olympic in the Pacific Coast finals."

—*LA Examiner*, December 19, 1938

First up was Big Boy, who had to dispose of San Francisco's Jack Lunny in a semi-final match, whilst Shorty awaited the result of Tony Pennisi (San Francisco) versus Ken Wren (Seattle).

According to a report by Bill Potts, the "tall, rangy and exceptionally clever" Lunny looked to be out-boxing Big Boy during the first round, but then made the mistake of going for the kill. Playing right into Big Boy's hands, Lunny found himself in the middle of a whirlwind from which he failed to extract himself. For the following three rounds, Lunny was raked with rights and lefts that put him in full retreat.

The twins were now just one step away from the national finals and their deciding bouts couldn't have been more different. Shorty looked on as Big Boy, in the second round of his final, was dropped to the canvas, and almost out of the ring, by Dale Maloney of Seattle. The right-hand punch from Maloney caught Big Boy with such force that he went through the ropes, onto the ring apron, and almost out into the stunned crowd. Big Boy appeared to struggle to his feet as referee Charley Randolph tolled off a count. Fighting back in the third round, Big Boy was rocked again by the power of Maloney's shots, but landed enough leather of his own to secure the stanza.

A superhuman effort was required by both boxers in the fourth and final round, Big Boy in order to pull out a win and Maloney to survive the onslaught. Local reporter Bill Potts wrote, "Hogue roared out for the final round with murder in his heart and hands a flying fan of leather." Maloney managed to remain upright, but appeared in bad shape as just about every punch from Big Boy sent him spinning from one corner of the ring to the next.

At the final bell both boxers appeared exhausted, especially Big Boy, who had already contested a semi-final bout that same evening. The decision was not altogether popular, as many in the gallery appeared to feel that Maloney had done enough — especially with the knockdown in the second round. However both judges and the referee cast their votes for Big Boy.

Shorty's final bout against Ken Wren, and the manner of the victory, appeared a little more emphatic — if less satisfactory. As both boys exchanged punches mid-ring Shorty uncorked a wicked left-hook which dropped Wren to the floor. Although he was up at the count of two, it seemed that his heavily bandaged knee would not support him and referee Jack Kennedy was forced to call a TKO victory for Shorty in the first round.

Another winner at the Pacific Coast tournament was Tommy Moyer of Portland, Oregon. Moyer (of the famous fighting family) had a successful amateur career — a reported 145 wins from 156 bouts — and almost made the USA Olympic team for the 1940 games. He was beaten in a box-off by one Sugar Ray Robinson. The two met at the Rochester New York Tournament of Champions on July 22, 1940, and the five round split decision verdict for Robinson was reported as being very close. When Robinson turned pro Moyer made the cut — only to see the games cancelled due to WWII. Moyer won a number of Pacific Coast titles as an amateur, and also won the AAU lightweight title in 1941. His younger brother Harry was runner-up in the 1934 tournament to Earl Booker (brother of Eddie Booker). Harry's sons, Denny and Phil Moyer, had successful professional careers in the 1950s and 60s, with both of them defeating the same Sugar Ray who had decisioned their uncle more than 20 years earlier.

. . .

A week after annexing the Pacific Coast titles the twins were in action again at the San Diego Coliseum; this time opposing each other:

> "In the three round feature exhibition between the Hogue twins, Willis and Willard, better known as 'Shorty' and 'Big Boy,' there was plenty of boxing displayed and a bit of comedy in which the incomparable Curley Morgan figured. The brothers put on quite a show, and in the second canto one of the twins, Curley is not sure which one, went down. In the third round the twin from the opposite corner went to the floor.
>
> Morgan was vexed no little when he discovered the boy who hit the canvas in the third was the same one who went down in the second, for the twins played a trick on the crowd by switching corners between rounds. It was lots of fun. "

> —*San Diego Evening Tribune*, December 12, 1938

After securing their places in the national finals — and having fun with Coliseum announcer Curley Morgan — the boys looked forward to their birthdays at the end of December. In typical twin fashion they decided to celebrate their 18th birthdays in an unconventional manner by entering a bull-riding contest. Their own slant on riding a bull was to mount it facing each other; they were thrown off seconds after coming out of the chute.

Burdette Kinne felt that both boys were destined to win national titles come January, 1939 because "the twins possess every weapon in the books for success. They hit hard with both fists, they are good defensive fighters and can analyze styles of fighting and they boast a courage and determination with which few fighters are blessed." Besides being strong, courageous and ring-wise, the boys also possessed great fitness:

"There was a mountain (in Jacumba) and every day they would run up that mountain; sometimes they would race. It was about a four-mile run, and that was up hill and down. And down was as hard as up. Then they work out on bags and sit-ups and other things. The big thing they had was each other, and not wanting the other to get ahead."

—Bob Dye

Jacumba is around 2,800 feet above sea level, and Jacumba Peak is 3,363 additional feet — as is 'Squaw Tit,' another local Jacumba mountain. This means that the twins were training at an altitude of around 1.2 miles. With El Centro and Brawley both below sea level (at minus 39 feet and minus 111 feet respectively) the twins were 'training and living high' and 'competing low' for much of their amateur careers. If their physiologies adapted to this kind of training, then they may well have had an advantage over their competitors with regard to the oxygen carrying capacity of their red blood cells. In other words, greater endurance.

On the night of the national Golden Gloves finals, the brothers lived up to home-town expectations. Big Boy outpointed Al Priest of Cambridge, Massachusetts (in the semi-final) before gaining the nod over Harold Smith of Detroit in the final of the 147-pound division. Shorty defeated local fighter James Toney in the semi-finals prior to smashing out a decision over New York's Vince Fratello in the 160-pound final.

The Jacumba residents were the only Pacific Coast representatives to annex national titles, but their victories helped the Pacific coast contingent win the team trophy for best overall performance. Paul Woods and Jimmy Lane both lost by a "flea's lip" in their finals, while Bee Jiminez and Henry De La Vega lost close semi-final bouts. Coach Art Martell also assisted Los Angeles flyweight Tommy Olivarri to a win in the finals. Olivarri was intent on entering the tournament, but was staying with his parents in Texas over the holidays, so he had to enter via the local tournament there.

The boys needed an extra suitcase to carry all the telegrams and congratulatory notes back to California. Shorty was quoted in the local press as saying, "Sure is swell to get all these wires. I didn't know we had so many friends until we won championships. They mus-ta' been Big Boy's friends." After winning the diamond belt titles at welterweight and middleweight, the Hogues were hot property and there was talk of movie deals. One film that did feature them was a Grantland Rice *"Sportlight"* short called *"Two of a Kind"*. The movie, narrated by Ted Husing, featured siblings in sport and included Joe and Dominic DiMaggio amongst others. The film was made in 1939 and released when the boys were moving up in the pro ranks.

Another 'Hollywood' connection Shorty had was the movie actress Nan Grey, who is probably best known for starring in *'Three Smart Girls"* (1936) and *'Three Smart Girls Grow Up"* with Deanna Durbin (1939) and *"Sea Spoilers"* (1936) with John Wayne. The starlet had a massive crush on Shorty, but he didn't appear to be interested.

The twins bade their final farewell to the amateur code on February 20 in a joint headliner at the San Diego Coliseum:

> "Shorty provided the final touch when, in the second round of his scheduled four-round battle with Luis Ruiz, Old Town welterweight, he lashed out with a series of terrific right uppercuts to score a technical knockout. Ruiz, a clever boxer, got through several stormy sessions in the first round, although a short, sharp right drove him to the canvas for a nine count just before the bell.
>
> In the second session Shorty put on an amazing exhibition of timing when he suddenly set up an attack that drove Ruiz clearly around the ring. Shorty hurled no less than a dozen

long and solid blows and didn't miss a one of them. Ruiz finally began bobbing under the straight rights, but Hogue put a stop to that and to his opponent as well. He just quickly switched tactics and brought up a sweeping uppercut to the chin which dropped Ruiz for a short count. Twice more the same blow put the Old Town boy on the floor, so referee John Perry stepped in and stopped proceedings.

Big Boy didn't have such an easy time, although he gave Bud Cramer, game Ocean Beach welterweight, a thorough beating. A right hand early in the first round had Cramer reclining on his back for a nine count, but he got up and made a fight of it the rest of the way. In the second heat a short right, delivered in close, sent the blood flowing from Cramer's nose, and although he rallied several times, he receipted for a good going over from then on. In the fourth, Big Boy turned on the heat, raised a "mouse" under Cramer's left eye and blasted him from corner to corner.

It was a polished performance that the twins put on and a fitting finish to their long careers in the amateurs. Their popularity was proven when more than 2,500 fans swarmed into the Coliseum to see them for the last time before turning professional."

—Ken Bojens, the *San Diego Union,* February 20, 1939

The twins had done just about all they could do as amateurs, and there seemed little incentive for them to remain as such. The professional game across the country appeared to be in a very healthy state.

THE RING magazine's world ratings for 1938 had Fred Apostoli, Solly Kreiger, Ron Richards, Walter Woods and Jock McAvoy in the top five at middleweight (the title was vacant at that time). The welterweight rankings listed Henry Armstrong as the world champion with Ernie Roderick, Fritzie Zivic, Charley Burley, Saverio Turiello and Sammy Luftspring all in contention. Joe Louis sat atop the heavyweights, and he had recently beaten out Henry Armstrong in a tie-breaker for THE RING magazine's 'Most Valuable Boxer' of 1938. The Brown Bomber also won the magazine's 'Merit Award':

"Just why the tie had to be broken against Armstrong will be indicated by the conditions which govern the poll for the Most Valuable Boxer. They follow below: —

1. Foremost in his contribution to the skill and science of boxing, not essentially as a champion.

2. Outstanding in combining with his leadership in the ring a high place as a sportsman.

3. Prominent in maintaining splendid public relations and beating down the constant effort to discredit the boxer as a citizen.

4. Unquestioned in associated with boxing skill and fine public reaction for clean and moral living.

5. Foremost as an example to the growing American boy.

It will be seen from perusal of these conditions that just so long as any doubt exists in the minds of the followers of boxing regarding the repudiated interview, Henry could not win the prize."

—*THE RING* April 1939

Armstrong had blotted his copybook in an interview with the press in California following the rescheduling of a title fight with Ceferino Garcia. According to an unnamed reporter, Henry had admitted to feigning an injury in order to obtain a postponement.

It was also reported that Armstrong denied the interview with the West Coast reporter had taken place, and there was documented evidence that a medical officer from the New York State Athletic Commission — who examined the champion — confirmed at the time that Armstrong had in fact injured his sacroiliac (hip).

Unfortunately, there was no getting away from the negative press concerning Armstrong's 'lie' about the injury. Whether it was true or not, the situation ended his chances of winning the award over Joe Louis.

Also according to their year end rankings for 1938, THE RING had a number of Californian fighters in the running for world honors: Lou Nova and Max Bear at heavyweight; Freddie Apostoli at middleweight; Chalky Wright at featherweight, and Jackie Zurich at flyweight.

Other West Coast fighters who appeared to be doing well at the time were Jackie Jurich, Little Dado, Joe Gavras, Harold Toussint, Eddie Booker, and Young Corbett (all San Jose), Tony Olivera, Al Manfredo and Danny LaVerne (San Francisco), Kenny LaSalle, Bobby Pacho, and Leon Zoritta (Los Angeles). While further up the coast in Washington, there was Tiger Jack Fox at light-heavyweight, Al Hostak, Freddie Steele and Allen Matthews at middleweight. The West Coast was stacked with great, young boxing talent, and with the Hogue twins' decision to enter the pro ranks, the talent pool was about to swell.

*Shorty defeats Sammy Nero in the LA Examiner Golden Gloves
(Hollywood Pic magazine - March 1940).*

The twins at the Main Street gym, LA (photo courtesy of Chuck Hasson)

ROUND 3

Minneapolis: Friday January 9, 1942

"In the third and fourth rounds it seemed the fight could go either way. It was a question which man would be the first to take the upper hand. Would Hogue's body punishment or Burley's sharp shots to the head be the first to turn the tide?"

—Dick Cullum, *Minneapolis Daily Times*

"Hogue drove a ripping right uppercut to Burley's groin in the fourth round, but the plucky negro didn't so much as complain to referee Gorman."

—George A. Barton, *Minneapolis Star Times*

CHAPTER FIVE

T he San Diego Coliseum at the southwest corner of 15th and E Streets would be the scene of the twins' professional debuts. The custom-made fight venue - the brainchild of Frank C. Higgins and Tommy Landis - first opened its doors on November 28, 1924. Linn Platner had promoted boxing there almost since the building's opening, and by the late 1930s and early '40s, his business was going good. There was regular wrestling on Tuesdays - though most of the real fight fans stayed away from such theatrics - and boxing on Fridays. There was definitely enough talent around to fill a fight card with six-rounders most Fridays. With tickets at 75 cents for general admission - going up to $1.10, $1.65 and $2.20 depending how close you wanted to be to ringside - the place could get full and raucous. Ladies were admitted free with escorts, so it was a cheap night out for a local ringworm and his gal or for a visiting sailor looking for entertainment. Most Fridays had enough action to warrant the attendance of the local press, with scribes from the *San Diego Union,* the *Evening Tribune,* the *San Diego Sun* and the *San Diego Independent* reporting on the action.

The Coliseum's interior and part of its arched roof had been badly damaged by a fire in April, 1938 - right about the time Archie Moore arrived from St Louis to try his luck on the West Coast. In his book *The Archie Moore Story* the Ol' Mongoose described his first meeting with San Diego's top promoter:

> "I never figured out what nationality Mr. Platner was, but he was American born, about forty-five, on the stout side and always well-dressed in a conservative manner. He had a swarthy complexion and a pleasant smile..."

According to his draft registration (1942), Linn Leroy Platner was born in Auburn, Indiana on August 13, 1894, so Archie Moore was close in his estimation of the promoter's age. The same registration document recorded him as being 5 feet 8 inches, 230 pounds, with brown eyes, brown hair, a dark complexion and tattoos on his forearms. Archie also said that from the moment he met the promoter at George Wilson's saloon, located on the corner opposite the Coliseum, he sensed right away that Platner's interests were "in fighters and the sport and that money was secondary." In order to keep the San Diego boxing scene alive during the brief crisis following the fire, Platner held promotions at Lane Field until the Coliseum was opened again. Archie Moore fought four times at Lane Field before headlining at the renovated arena on September 2, 1938, when he would face off against Johnny (Bandit) Romero.

Six months after Moore's first appearance at the Coliseum, the Hogue twins made their debuts at the same venue - headlining a card on March 3, 1939. Shorty made quick work of Al Jiminez in his professional debut, scoring a third round kayo. Big Boy had to be content with a points win over six rounds.

Platner featured the twins together again as attractions on their second pro card, a pattern which, as we shall see, he repeated over and over. This time, Shorty made even quicker work of his opponent than in his first fight, dispatching Hut Thompson in just one minute 15 seconds of the first round. Big Boy again was forced to travel the scheduled six-round distance in winning a decision over Bobby Espinosa. To be fair, it should be noted that Big Boy's foes on each card had posted better winning percentages than those of Shorty.

Not surprisingly, word of the twins' prowess traveled up the coast to Los Angeles where Olympic Auditorium matchmaker Tom Galley promised a tough night's work for both boys:

"Tom Galley had more trouble making matches for the Hogue Twins, who top the card at the Olympic Auditorium tomorrow night, than he did with the Joe Louis-Jack Roper bout for the world's heavyweight championship.

The Hogues, who appear in a twin-six wind-up, wanted what is known in ring parlance as 'soft touches.' Galley insisted on real opposition — and it was Galley who won the argument.

Willis (Shorty) Hogue will tangle tails with Ray Vargas, Mexican middleweight, whose right hand has dropped such good boys as Al Romero and Tommy Hart to the canvas.

Willard (Big Boy) Hogue faces Davey Chacon, a fast-moving, rapid-fire puncher.

Tomorrow's battles mark the third appearance of the Hogues as professionals. They had two fights apiece in San Diego, winning impressively. However, the caliber of their opposition didn't measure up to Vargas and Chacon."

—*LA Times*, March 13, 1939

The tougher opposition of Vargas and Chacon meant that both twins were forced to go the distance, and both remained undefeated. Ten days after going six hard rounds with Ray Vargas, Shorty was given the opportunity to gain revenge over the last man to best him as an amateur - Miller Fonseca. After Big Boy knocked out George Romero in one round, Shorty took Fonseca apart in three. Once again, Shorty could boast he had beaten every man he had ever faced.

The boys would pile a staggering five fights each into their first month as professional fighters, with four of those fights taking place at the Coliseum. At the onset of April 1939, Shorty was 5-0 with four knockouts and Big Boy was 5-0 with two knockouts. Although Shorty had enjoyed more success in the amateur ranks (at the same time intensifying Big Boy's envy), he was about to be the first to stumble as a professional.

On April 10 at Ocean Park in Santa Monica, Big Boy defeated Les 'Red' Green, aka *The Signal Kid* on points over six rounds, while Shorty was stopped by former 175-pound Diamond Belt winner Tommy Garland via a TKO (cut eye) in three. The loss put the boys out of sync with each other as Big Boy fought at San Diego just four days later while Shorty took two weeks off for his cut to heal. All of their initial professional showings had been on the same bill.

Losing to Garland was disappointing to Shorty, but no disgrace because Garland was regarded as a top prospect, and the fight took place on his home turf. Gabrielle (Hap) Navarro, one-time Hollywood Stadium publicity director, recalled that, "Garland was one of the most popular fighters to ever show at Ocean Park back in my day. In fact, Garland preceded Artie Aragon as the local press nominee for the 'Golden Boy' label in California." An account written two days after the fight by LA Times sportswriter Bob Ray supports Navarro's recollection:

> "Tommy Garland, the kid who stopped "Shorty" Hogue the other eve at Ocean Park, is said to be one of the best-looking

fistic prospects to come along here in some time. Ancil Hoffman, the manager of the Baers', intimated that he might like to buy Garland's contract even before he'd stopped Hogue. Hoffman saw Garland work in the gym and liked his looks."

—*LA Times*, April 12, 1939

Garland's popularity was helped by the fact that he also had movie-star looks. As an actor in Hollywood Garland later appeared in a number of boxing-based movies including: *Golden Boy* (1939), *Knockout* (1941), *Right Cross* (1950), *The Harder They Fall*, and *Somebody Up There Likes Me* (1956).

By the time Shorty next entered the ring, he was a married man. The marriage was a spur-of-the-moment decision made as the pair drove across the border to Arizona where they obtained a couple of witnesses and a license. A report in the local press provide details on the affair:

"Miss Verna Mae Palmer, daughter of Mr & Mrs W.L. Palmer of 361 Holt Ave, El Centro, and Willis 'Shorty' Hogue, son of Mr & Mrs Glenn C. Briggs of Jacumba, exchanged marriage vows here Tuesday afternoon. The 4 o'clock ceremony was solomnized in the Methodist church with the Reverend W.L. Summer officiating."

—*Yuma Daily Sun & Arizona Sentinel*, April 14, 1939

The newlyweds had plans to head for New York for the World's Fair a couple of weeks later. The truth of the matter was that they were just two crazy kids — the bride only 15 years old and the groom barely 18. Shorty couldn't stand for his sibling to have anything he didn't. According to Bob Dye, Verna could be a handful:

> "Once when Shorty came to Porterville with his new wife Verna Mae, he wanted to take her rabbit hunting, about 3 miles from my folks place. My brother had a 22 rifle, but I did not have one, so Shorty took me to town and bought me one. Also, that would give his wife one to use while she was here.
>
> My brother and I went with them to Lewis Hill where the rabbits were. When we got there Verna went in the orange orchard, and she saw a dog and took a shot at it, and someone was right by the dog. And boy did he start screaming and we started running. We got in the car, and went home and that was the end of the rabbit hunting. But I got a new .22 rifle thanks to Verna. Verna was a wild and very, very pretty blond."

—Bob Dye

While Shorty enjoyed his wedding in Yuma, Big Boy took on Kenny Reed in San Diego (on the same day). He was also the first of the twins to have a write-up in *THE RING* magazine:

> "Big Boy Hogue, 146, Jacumba, scored his eighth consecutive win when he decisioned the veteran Kenny Reed in the six-round main event at San Diego on April 14. Hogue, the smaller of the famous twins, won five of the six rounds.
>
> In the six-round semi-windup, Sammy O'Dell Mason, 160, Los Angeles, stopped Dick Richie, 156, San Diego, in the third round."

—*THE RING*, July 1939

Just two weeks after the loss to Garland, and two weeks after exchanging marriage vows, Shorty came storming back to stop Sammy O'Dell Mason in San Diego (scoring three knockdowns in the 6th). A week later, he met Karl Lester in San Diego:

"The famous fighting twins of Jacumba, Shorty and Big Boy Hogue, still continue to win their bouts. In the featured contests at the San Diego Coliseum, Big Boy Hogue scored a four-round KO over Angus Smith, negro boxer of Santa Barbara, and Shorty won a hard-fought six-round decision over Karl Lester of Pacific Beach".

—*THE RING*, August 1939

The boys were back in tandem with both winning again at the Coliseum on May 12. Big Boy defeated Uli Harris over six rounds on May 15, then Shorty damaged his hand outpointing Hugie Wyatt on May 19, putting him out of action for close to six weeks. During Shorty's recovery period, Big Boy had four fights for four wins and was still unbeaten in 14 starts:

"Linn Platner, San Diego promoter, used Big Boy Hogue, smaller of the Hogue twins, in three of his four Coliseum AC main events this month [June]. Results of the San Diego fights are as follows: Big Boy Hogue, 146, stopped Johnny Verdusco, 141, in the third; Big Boy Hogue, 147, scored a TKO over Jack Rainwater, 150, in the first round; Big Boy Hogue won over Jesse James Jackson, 141, in six rounds."

—*THE RING*, September 1939

The win over Jackson was revenge for Big Boy, having lost to him only five months previously as an amateur. The *Nevada State Journal*

(June 17) reported that Big Boy had a 4-1/4-pound weight pull over Jackson and handed out a sound beating. In preparation for Vedusco, Rainwater and Jackson, Big Boy had to modify his training:

"Big Boy Hogue has a new wrinkle, company for road work.

No one enjoys rambling at a dog trot over roads, trail or anything else, just as a conditioning manoeuvre. In fact, in boxing today road work is almost becoming a lost art, though it is one of the most important parts of proper conditioning.

The Jacumba welter usually has his twin brother, Shorty, to run with for company. But of late with Shorty on vacation he's had to do his mountain running by himself. But no more. Big Boy found himself a bulldog pal in El Centro and in the space of a few days has trained him to accompany him on runs.

'It works out swell too.', says Big Boy. 'I get tired by afternoon and take a nap when I'm training. Now that the dog runs up the hills with me, he gets tired, too, and will sleep when I do in the afternoons.'"

—*San Diego Union*, June, 8 1939

A week after beating Jackson on June 16 Big Boy defeated the veteran Bobby Pacho over 10 rounds in El Centro (June 22). Shorty beat Carmen Georgino at the same venue the following week. Big Boy's win over Pacho was seen as something of an upset as only a week previously Pacho had defeated the highly-touted Glen Lee. Going into the fight, Pacho also had more draws on his record (won 81-lost 50-drawn 15) than Big Boy had total fights. Pacho had fought them all — Henry Armstrong, Eddie Booker, Kid Azteca, Turkey Thompson, Fred Apostoli, Ceferino Garcia, Tony Canzoneri,

Fritzie Zivic — you name them, and the Arizona native had been in with the cream of world boxing and was never disgraced.

As the twins would pack most local arenas when they were on the bill, it made sense from a promotional standpoint to have them fight alternate weeks. In their first year as professional fighters, the twins appeared on the same bill 13 times, but more recently they were headlining as separate drawing cards. On July 1, 1939, Big Boy defeated Ray Vargas over six rounds, and the following week Shorty beat Jimmy Gleason via the same route. On July 9, the boys boxed an exhibition at an event to host the Imperial Valley Peace Officers in Jacumba. Five days later Shorty was in action again, this time going up against Homer Slack. Shorty had the added bonus of being assisted in his preparations for Slack by none other than future boxing legend Archie Moore. At the time, Archie was just a recent arrival on the San Diego fight scene:

> "In preparing for tomorrow night's six-round main event at the Coliseum with Homer Slack, Shorty Hogue, Jacumba middleweight, has been working out daily with Archie Moore, clever St. Louis negro boxer.
>
> The latter, who gained national ranking by beating Marty Simmons and giving Teddy Yarosz a close engagement, is said to have helped Shorty considerably in learning new ring maneuvers."
>
> —*San Diego Union,* July 13, 1939

Evidently, Moore's assistance was a big help as Shorty scored an impressive technical knockout over Slack in one minute and 26 seconds of the fourth round. As it happened, the lessons he learned from Archie would hold him in good stead when they fought each other later in the year.

· · ·

The twins were together again as co-features at the Coliseum on July 28. Big Boy outpointed Al Smith over six rounds and Shorty repeated the trick against Johnny Folio of West Virginia. Big Boy was the solo main event the following week, defeating Chuey Vargas over six rounds. During the build-up to a fight with Jackie Taylor - scheduled for August 11 - Shorty had a health scare:

> **"EL CENTRO**, *Aug 4*—Shorty Hogue of the Jacumba fight twins was discharged from a local hospital today. He had been under observation following an attack of appendicitis. Physicians decided an operation was now not necessary."

> —*LA Times,* August 5, 1939

Apparently recovered by August 11, Shorty disposed of Jackie Taylor in one round. Big Boy repeated his earlier win over Chuey Vargas on the same bill. A week later, the twins were in action again:

> "Shorty Hogue, who likes nothing better than to wade in and trade wallops with an opponent, won't have to wait long to engage in his favourite pastime when he meets Jimmy Brott, good-looking Riverside middleweight, in the first half of a double six-round event at the Coliseum Athletic Club Friday night.

> In Brott, Shorty, the heavier of the two Jacumba Hogue twins, will be tackling probably the hardest hitter of his career. Although he is green and unable to keep up with smart boxers, Brott packs a terrific punch and is equally accurate either to the head or body. Several times in appearances here, he has appeared to be in trouble, but he has a habit of suddenly lashing out with hard rights to the body, and the manoeuvre takes quick effect.

Unlike his brother, Big Boy, Shorty does not rely greatly on his defence to win bouts, but prefers to open up and rough things up a bit. Strong and invariably well-conditioned, he is able to do that with the ordinary run of fighters, but he will find his work cut out for him when he squares off with Brott.

The other main event, between Big Boy Hogue and Al Smith, is a rematch in which Hogue will be trying to demonstrate conclusively that he is the better man. The last time they fought Smith gave Big Boy all the leather he could handle, and, although the latter was given the decision, there were enough dissenters in the crowd to bring on demands for another meeting."

—*San Diego Union*, August 15, 1939

On the night of the fight, both Shorty and Big Boy dominated their opponents. Down at the end of the first round, Brott was saved by the bell. When he went down again in the second, his corner threw in the towel, but referee Steve Nyland ignored it. Shorty was waved in and dropped the defenceless Brott again with a swift 'one-two' - this time Nyland had seen enough and called an end to the fight. Big Boy had Al Smith on the canvas three times in the fifth round, but could not find the finishing punch.

The boys were signed up to fight again the following week (August 25) - Shorty versus Carlos Garcia and Big Boy versus Jesse James Jackson. The day before the fight Big Boy was following a trend set by Shorty when he went through a workout with Archie Moore at the Coliseum Athletic Club. In a final hard drill for his six-round rematch with Jackson, Big Boy had his hands full with Moore for the entire duration of the three-round tussle. Archie's feinting, rolling style baffled Hogue in the first round as Moore out-jabbed him on the outside and tied him up in the clinches, but before the round ended Big Boy began to figure out Archie's attack.

According to local press reports, the second and third rounds of the workout were better than most regular ring matches as the pair tossed punches from all angles. Previously, Big Boy had no problem handling opponents at in-fighting since that game was meat and potatoes for both he and Shorty. Against the more experienced and heavier Moore however, Big Boy found that he couldn't use his natural strength to maneuver the St. Louis man around for inside punches. One scribe present at the session wrote that Big Boy was forced to "... *keep busy protecting himself*" instead. Obviously frustrated with his lack of success, Big Boy started to charge aggressively at Moore, who easily avoided the rushes. On one occasion, Big Boy charged a little too hard while Moore side-stepped him and watched as Big Boy went through the ropes and out into the ringside seats.

To prepare for his fight, Shorty sparred two fast rounds with with local light-heavyweight Don Junk and one each with Burton Rogers and another amateur boxer.

The twins' hard work in training proved to be worth the effort. Shorty comfortably beat Garcia the following night - via kayo in four rounds - while Big Boy had to put in a strong, come-from-behind finish to get the nod over Jesse James Jackson. A cut over the right eye kept him out of action for several weeks.

In its 'Sports Postscripts' column (August 29, 1939), the *LA Times*, under the headline *SAN DIEGO LIKES THE HOGUES,* published the following:

"Shorty Hogue and his little brother, Big Boy (Shorty's a middleweight and Big Boy a welter) are making weekly stands at San Diego ... or almost. They fight at El Centro sometimes, too, but up this way promoters haven't been able to get 'em booked for one reason or another.

The Hogues are getting cocky over their string of victories. Some say they have a right to be that way ... they're going places ... especially Big Boy. Others shake their heads.

They pick off about $500 a show at San Diego between them. Enough to buy a pair of cream-colored roadsters and keep the payment up. Remember how Max Baer used to like the flashy gas buggies?"

Shorty purchased a very bright yellow Chevy coup - the problem was he had no experience of driving. By his own (later) admission, he was involved in a number of traffic accidents when young, apparently a result of fast and careless driving. Family members have stated that the twins seemed to have no fear whatsoever, and often wondered if they even felt physical pain. Big Boy was also involved in a number of driving accidents, one occurring just three days before the above report appeared and including his nephew Richard Plummer. Big Boy's vehicle collided with one driven by a Delbert Lowry at Arnold and Landis Streets in San Diego. Fortunately, no one was seriously hurt, though the accident appears to have kept Big Boy out of action the following week of September 8.

Since his loss to Garland (April 10) Shorty had won 11 on the spin and had stopped more than half of his opponents. No doubt buoyed by his recent successes, he took a second fight with Tommy Garland in San Diego on September 8. Again the slashing fists of the Ocean Park light-heavyweight halted any plans for revenge that Shorty may have had since the bout was stopped due to cuts in the second round. It was Shorty's first professional loss in front of his hometown fans.

With family pride at stake, Big Boy put out a challenge to the naturally heavier Garland, and only a week after the win over Shorty

Hogue, Garland found himself in the same San Diego ring opposing Big Boy:

> "Garland had an interesting feud going with the incomparable Hogue twins, my all-time favorite tandem of fighting sibs. The Hogues' had a personal fetish - if a fighter whipped one of them, that guy could sure as hell expect to be challenged by the other Hogue twin. Sometimes the loss was avenged, but that didn't matter much. The Hogue high was in getting in a few licks in reprisal, and they usually did. When Tommy Garland won over Shorty Hogue, the better of the two brothers, Big Boy Hogue spotted him several pounds and defeated Tommy."

> —Gabrielle 'Hap' Navarro

In his usual *'In Sunny California'* section of THE RING, respected scribe Harry Winkler summed up recent happenings for the Hogue boys - including Shorty's rubber match with Tommy Garland - and provided a little insight for those fighters eyeing the apparent rich pickings on the coast:

> "The writer of this column receives many letters from negro boxers who are desirous of coming to Southern California, therefore I deem it my duty to inform all colored boxers contemplating a trip to these parts that they will find it tough sledding out here.

> There is but one club in Los Angeles where the colored boxers can appear, and there are dozens of negro boxers in the city who cannot secure enough bouts to make a living. If this statement is doubted, I suggest that the skeptical parties write

to either Jackie Wilson, Big Boy Brey, Georgie Crouch, Chalky Wright, Eddie Booker, Lloyd Marshall, Archie Moore, Yancey Henry, Henry Woods, or a dozen other first-class colored boxers who are familiar with the conditions.

San Diego – Shorty Hogue of Jacumba, larger of the fighting twins, had his winning streak brought to an end by Tommy Garland of Ocean Park, who stopped him in the second round. Each weighed 158.

Ocean Park – the Hogue twins, Shorty and Big Boy, both scored wins in a double main event at the Ocean Park Arena. Shorty, 160, decisioned Tommy Garland, 160 in six, and Big Boy, 147, laced Babe Hernandez, 148, in six, scoring two knockdowns over the Mexican."

—*THE RING*, December 1939

Big Boy would have no doubt kidded Shorty that he softened Garland up for him during his own six-round victory, but a win was a win. Shorty was finally able to get the victory he craved along with the ability to boast that he had still beaten every man he had faced.

On October 6 it was Big Boy's turn to have his perfect record tarnished as he drew over six rounds with Johnny Freitas, though he could probably be excused the momentary lapse as his second child (Sherry) was born the same day. Shorty won on the same bill versus Art Johnson, posting another six-round points win.

Shorty won his next two fights in October 1939, against Marine Saxell and Billy Mitchell (both by six-round decisions), before taking time out with recurring hand problems. Big Boy fought once more in October - beating Nick Massiello over six rounds at the San Diego Coliseum.

Meanwhile, three-time world champion Henry Armstrong had

been busy. Between January and May of 1939, he successfully defended his 147-pound welterweight crown five times with victories over Baby Arizmendi, Bobby Pacho, Lew Feldman, Davey Day and Ernie Roderick. In August, he lost his 135-pound world light-weight title to Lew Ambers in 15 rounds at New York, but the defeat was of relatively little consequence because the welterweight and 126-pound featherweight titles were not at risk, and his string of five successful welterweight title defenses in as many months overshadowed the loss of the lightweight crown. Even so, Armstrong was not done with 1939, for he was about to go on an even more amazing run that would make his prior accomplishments for the year look pale by comparison.

On October 9, he scored a four-round knockout over Al Manfredo in Des Moines; on the 13th, he kayoed Howard Scott in two rounds at Minneapolis; on the 20th, he stopped Richie Fontaine in three sessions at Seattle; on the 24th, he won a 10-round decision from Jimmy Garrison at Los Angeles; and on the 30th, he knocked out Bobby Pacho in the fourth round at Denver. Thus ended October 1939, a month in which he defended his title five times in four weeks, a concentrated string of successful title defenses that likely will never be surpassed. Before the year ended, Armstrong added another title defense to his record, bringing his tally for the year to 11 wins, one loss, and nine knockouts. All 11 wins were successful welterweight title defenses. The sole defeat was the controversial decision loss to Ambers.

Armstrong registered more than just one good winning run in his career. While 1939 is impressive due to the number of title defences his accomplishments in 1937 are also hard to beat. Starting the year on January 1 and ending it on December 12 (his 25th birthday), Armstrong fought at least once every month and scored 26 knock-outs in 27 fights - winning the featherweight title from Petey Sarron along the way. The only man to last the distance with "Homicide Hank" was Aldo Spoldi of New York (via Lombardia, Italy).

. . .

Big Boy Hogue continued his winning ways throughout November 1939 by beating Billy Mitchell, Jimmy Johnson and Tabby Romero on consecutive Fridays at the San Diego Coliseum. On December 8, Big Boy took on local fighter Herman Graves - also at the Coliseum:

> "Big Boy Hogue of nearby Jacumba, undefeated since he joined the professional ranks a year ago, chalked up another triumph last night when he slashed out a technical knockout victory over Bomber Graves, El Centro. Calif., in the third-round of a scheduled six round main event.
>
> Graves held his own for the first two rounds but in the third canto Big Boy caught his foe with a smashing left hook to the chin which rendered Graves helpless. The end came after two minutes and 30 seconds of the third round. Hogue weighed 157 and Graves 154."

—*Modesto Bee,* December 9, 1939

Big Boy then signed for a match with the heavy-handed Elbert (Turkey) Thompson to take place on December 26. Just to make things more difficult, it was set for the date of his 20th birthday. With sibling rivalry seemingly at an all-time high, Shorty decided to go one better and signed to fight a previous training partner — the dangerous young middleweight Archie Moore.

Prior to their fights with Thompson and Moore, it was announced in the *Knockout* magazine (December 23, 1939) that the twins had found themselves a manager - George Barnett of San Diego.

The twins' nephew Bob Dye, recalled listening to Big Boy's fight against Thompson on the radio. Thompson, an Oklahoma boy, was a year and a day older than Big Boy, having been born on Christmas Day 1919 (hence the name 'Turkey'). Thompson had lost only two of 16 fights coming into the Hogue bout, both to Bobby Seaman, one of which had been an apparent robbery (Thompson had also beaten Seaman twice). His biggest win to date had been a furious encounter with Bobby Pacho the previous September.

Unfortunately for Big Boy, the Thompson fight proved to be a significant setback. The *Fresno Bee* called it " . . . a slugfest from the first bell." An article by THE RING correspondent furnished a particularly succinct, but accurate description of the action:

> "Turkey Thompson, Los Angeles negro, scored two K.O. victories over Hogue, but referee Benny Whitman reneged on the first one. Thompson had Hogue against the ropes, stunned from a terrific right to the chin in the first round. Hogue dropped his hands and started for his corner, in what appeared to be 'retiring.'
>
> Referee Whitman raised Thompson's hand, and the fight seemed to be over, but out came Hogue from his corner, claiming that he thought the bell had rung, ending the round. So Whitman called Thompson back, explained the situation to the crowd and ordered the bout continued. Thompson floored Hogue twice in the second and finished him early in the third."

—*THE RING*, February 1940

The loss was Big Boy's first in 30 bouts. In 1940 alone, Thompson would prove his credentials as one of the better fighters on the West Coast with victories over Johnny (Bandit) Romero, Teddy Yarosz and Glen Lee.

Three days after Big Boy's loss to Thompson, Shorty fought Archie Moore at the San Diego Coliseum. Prior to the bout, Archie had dropped only three decisions in 44 fights and had scored 28 knock-outs. A sampling of news reports from ringside provides an idea of how close the fight was:

> "San Diego —Shorty Hogue upset the dope by gaining a six-round decision over the classy Archie Moore in a fast, hard-fought contest. Moore boxed beautifully, but the rugged Hogue would not give the clever negro a chance to get set, tearing in and swinging all the way. Hogue weighed 160, Moore, 158."

> —*THE RING*, March 1940

> "Although Hogue received the decision from the referee, most spectators thought it was a draw. Moore was penalized the fifth round because of low blows. This cost Moore the fight, as he would have won that round. Hogue bored in, both hands flailing, and Archie tried to keep the action at long range."

> —*San Diego Union*, December 30, 1939

While the journalist for the *Knockout* (13 January, 1940) wrote that Shorty's win was a surprise, he also reported that Shorty " ... rushed Moore off his feet to win a deserved decision." The writer also claimed that the gate — $2,500 — was probably the biggest of the year at the Coliseum.

Many years later, Moore admitted he was so disgusted he briefly contemplated retirement. Fortunately for the boxing world, he decided to carry on, but was looking much further afield than California. Hooking up with fight manager Jack Richardson, Archie headed for the Antipodes and a series of bouts against the best that Australia had to offer.

Come the last day of December, 1939, the twins had amassed an astonishing 55 professional fights between them. Big Boy held a slight edge with a record of 28 wins, one loss and one draw, while Shorty had recorded 22 wins and two losses. In the 10 months they had been punching-for-pay, one or both of them engaged in three or more fights per month on seven different occasions. They had appeared on the same bill together a total of 13 times, with Shorty winning all his fights when they appeared in tandem, and Big Boy winning 12 and drawing one.

According to the *San Diego Union* (March 6, 1940), 1939 had been an especially big year for the smaller Hogue twin. The paper's boxing writer wrote that, "Big Boy's slate of wins and losses for the first year in boxing is just about a record." The same report estimated that he had earned about $4,000 gross from his 31 fights.

THE RING magazine again voted Joe Louis as the 'Fighter of the Year' in addition to presenting him with their *'Merit Award'* for the second successive year. The so-called "Bible of Boxing' also handed out awards for 'Classiest Fighter' — Billy Conn, 'Knockout King' — Pat Cominsky (with 16 of 20 fights ending early), 'Largest Individual Money-Maker for 1939' — Joe Louis (who made $303,455 for four Heavyweight Championship defences) and 'Most Active Fighter' — Tommy Speigal, who had engaged in 28 fights. Someone obviously lost sight of Big Boy Hogue.

The magazine also tabbed Vic Dellicurti (New York) and Turkey Thompson (Los Angeles) as the prospects of the year among the middleweights and bestowed the same honor upon Mike Kaplan (Boston) and Maxie Berger (Montreal) at welterweight.

The twins going through their paces (above and below)
for the Hollywood Pic magazine photographer (March 1940)

Frances and Big Boy out at the movies with Virginia and Shorty
(Hollywood Pic magazine - March 1940)

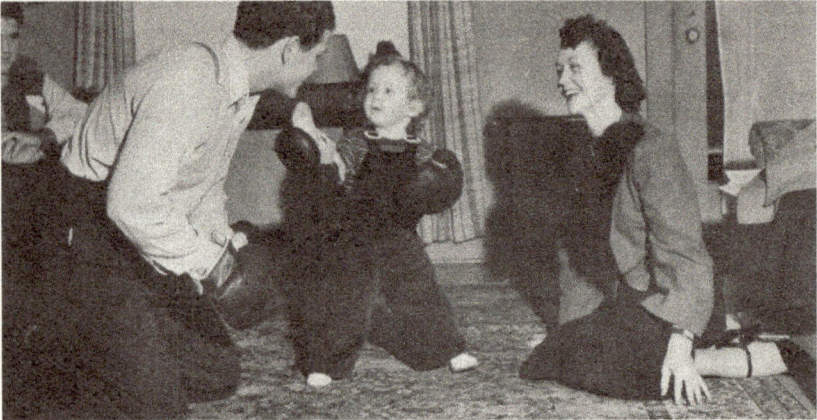

Big Boy, Jimmie, and Frances Hogue
(Hollywood Pic magazine - March 1940)

ROUND 4

Minneapolis: Friday January 9, 1942

"At the end of the fourth round it appeared that the bulldog character of Hogue's attack might weaken his man before Burley's sniping could check the determined charges."

—Dick Cullum, *Minneapolis Daily Times*

CHAPTER SIX

Big Boy was the first of the twins to see action in 1940, defeating Baby Face Robinson over six rounds in January. Also in January, Shorty took on the experienced Bobby Pacho:

> "Shorty Hogue pounded out a decisive victory over Bobby Pacho in a 10-rounder at the Coliseum. Hogue was credited with eight of the rounds."

> —*THE RING*, April 1940

Shorty was back in action just seven days later (January 19), meeting Charlie Simpson at the San Diego Coliseum. According to Harry E. Winkler of THE RING Shorty, administered "a severe lacing" to Charlie 'Suitcase' Simpson. Winkler also reported that Simpson didn't take a round, though Shorty was unable to put him down:

> **"SAN DIEGO**, *Jan 20* - Scheduled to fight Johnny Nelson, Shorty Hogue, one half of the Jacumba battling twin

combination, instead met Suitcase Simpson, 162, Los Angeles and copped a ten-round main event decision here last night. Hogue won every round from Simpson whose services were enlisted when it was learned Nelson was suffering from a cold."

—Fresno Bee, Jan 20, 1940

THE RING also reported that Shorty was seeking a match with Turkey Thompson "to avenge his brother's defeat." Harry Winkler pondered such a match and wondered who would be left to avenge Shorty's defeat should the bout take place.

The previously ailing Johnny Nelson was in finer fettle the following week when he accepted a second opportunity to tangle with Shorty at the Coliseum. After defeating Nelson via a ten-round points decision on January 26 and contesting three fights in 14 days, Shorty and Verna Mae had their marriage annulled due to her being under age at the time of the original ceremony. It seemed that Shorty could not bear to be any different to his brother, and less than two weeks later (February 7, 1940), he applied for a license in order to marry Virginia Rigby. Again Shorty lied about his age (claiming to be 22), and Virginia claimed to be 18. Whatever their ages, the wedding appeared to be a distraction that kept him out of competition for the whole of February.

After almost six weeks off, Big Boy was signed up to meet Los Angeles middleweight Jimmy Casino in San Diego the following month. During the build up to the six-rounder at the Coliseum, the San Diego Union reported on the twins' latest training regimen. Instead of the regular, monotonous, running routine the twins set out a trap line in the hills around Jacumba. Big Boy told the paper he didn't expect to get wealthy doing it, but that it might serve as a decent income if they could catch enough fur-bearing animals. The real bonus for the boys were the miles they both clocked up checking the traps several times a day.

The same report (February 15, 1940) also made a point of highlighting the twins' new look. Shorty had decided he wanted some warts removed from his scalp, so the curly locks had to go. Since both boys were proud of the fact that their fans had difficulty telling them apart, the twins decided Big Boy should follow suit.

As for the upcoming fight, Casino was viewed as no worse than even money to win a decision over Big Boy. Supporting such odds was the fact that Jimmy had a victory over Bobby Seamon, who held a win over Turkey Thompson. Casino was also judged to have faced a better class of opposition to Big Boy while amassing a 26-4-4 record. According to the May edition of THE RING, "Casino was best at long range, but Hogue punished Jimmy when in close. Both resorted to rough tactics." After six rounds of scrapping, there appeared to be little to separate the two, and the result was a draw.

After marrying for the second time - and taking two months off - Shorty was intent on making up for lost time with three bouts in March, all points wins. Big Boy had two bouts, winning over Sammy O'Dell Mason and losing on a cut to Jimmy Casino in a rematch. The win over Mason came the same day Big Boy's trapping line experiment literally came back to bite him. The *San Diego Union* reported:

"The West is still wild. If you don't think so, consult Big Boy Hogue. He can offer proof.

The Jacumba boxer had a line of traps in the mountains near his Jacumba home. Last Friday, the day of his bout with O'Dell Mason at the Coliseum, Big Boy ran his line of traps before coming to the arena to weigh in. He found a coyote snared in one. In trying to muzzle the animal, the boxer got his hand too near the coyote's mouth and received a deep tooth wound in one finger."

Shorty's victories came over the veteran Johnny (Bandit) Romero, Bobby Pacho and Jimmy Casino - revenge for the Hogue family name and more evidence to prove to Big Boy who was the better fighter.

The win over Johnny Romero, whom Shorty spotted 11 pounds, is an indication of the skill level he had achieved after only 13 months in the pro game. The 30-tear-old Bandit, who had been in the game since 1928, was a veteran of 138 recorded professional fights, the majority of which had taken place in San Diego. Most importantly, his list of opponents read like a 'Who's Who' of boxing, with names such as Ralph Chong, Ceferino Garcia, Gorilla Jones, Freddie Steele, Swede Berglund, Gus Lesnevich, Al Gainer, Red Bruce, Lloyd Marshall and Archie Moore were scattered throughout his glittering record. Romero's win over Moore (June 24, 1938) was Archie's first on the West Coast and only his second loss in 27 fights.

In March, 1940 the twins featured in a three-page spread of the *Hollywood Pic* magazine. Big Boy appeared on the cover along with photographs of Miss England and Hollywood starlet Anne Sheridan. The feature in the popular magazine also appeared at the time the twins were celebrating the anniversary of their first year in the professional ranks. By the end of March 1940, Shorty had been in the ring 31 times, and Big Boy an incredible 35 times.

The boys continued apace until April 1940, with Big Boy starting the month off with another win over Baby Face Robinson. Shorty kept up by defeating Bandit Romero again:

"In San Diego—Shorty Hogue 158, repeated his win over Johnny (Bandit) Romero, 168, in a fast eight-rounder at the

Coliseum. The fight was very close at the end of the seventh, but Hogue belted the veteran southpaw plenty in the final round to cinch (sic) the decision."

—*THE RING,* July 1940

THE RING reporter, Harry Winkler, failed to mention that Shorty scored a knockdown in the fifth round. Something that Mr. Winkler did report in the same edition of the magazine, was a list of California's top fighters in each division:

"In answer to the many requests I receive for such information, I am herewith listing the names of three boxers in each weight division whom I consider as being the best in California at these weights:

112—Little Pancho, Manuel Ortiz, Jackie Jurich (Of course Little Dado would be listed here if he could make the weight, which is doubtful).

118—Little Dado, Tony Olivera, Horace Mann (There is little doubt but what Pancho can beat Mann, but I am listing each boxer in only one weight).

126—Verne Bybee, Richie Lemos, Chick Delaney (Chalky Wright, a California boy, is not listed here because he has made New York his home in the last year).

135—Jackie Wilson, George Latka, Toby Virgil (A number of good opponents for these three, namely Garrison, Crouch and Chavez, cannot make the lightweight limit).

147—Henry Armstrong, Eddie Booker, Jimmy Garrison (I rate Garrison here, although a 140-pounder, because I can think of no third California 147-pound-er (with Leon Zoritta in Australia) who can beat him).

160—Ceferino Garcia, Turkey Thompson, Lloyd Marshall.

175—Jack Coggins, Pat Valentino, Johnny (Bandit) Romero.

Heavyweight—Lou Nova, Buddy Baer, Max Baer

(True, the present ability of Nova and Baer is unknown, but I cannot believe that either of them would be beaten by such other California heavies such as Chuck Crowell, Bob Nestell, Big Boy Bray or Sonny Boy Walker)."

—*THE RING*, July 1940

Winkler's ranking of Bandit Romero at number three in the light-heavyweight division is interesting, given the fact that Shorty Hogue (basically an overblown welterweight) had beaten him twice. If the magazine's California correspondent had ranked Shorty anywhere amongst the middleweights, his high ranking of Romero would seem less puzzling.

Also in the July 1940 edition of *THE RING* (*p48*) Eddie Borden, author of the column *"A Corner in the Fistic Market,"* listed the California-based contenders in Winkler's list as he viewed them in the world rankings of the top-ten in each division:

- *112*—Manuel Ortiz (number 3)
- *118*—Little Dado (1), Tony Olivera (3), Chick Delaney(10)
- *126*—Verne Bybee (9)
- *135*—Jackie Wilson(3), George Latka (4),
- *147*—Henry Armstrong (Champion)
- *160*—Ceferino Garcia (1), Lloyd Marshall (8)
- *175*— Turkey Thompson (6)
- *Heavyweight*—Buddy Baer (5)

Borden also ranked Archie Moore – most likely missing from Winkler's rankings due to his campaigning in the Antipodes – at number five among the middleweights.

Two weeks after his second victory over Romero (April 26), Shorty forced referee Steve Nyland to intervene in the seventh round of his bout with Angelo Puglisi at the Coliseum. On the same night, Big Boy stopped Nick Massiello in five on the undercard of 'California' Jackie Wilson vs Tony Chavez in Hollywood, making Wilson the first black fighter to headline at the Legion Stadium.

On May 10 at the San Diego Coliseum, Shorty stopped Petey Mike in the second of a scheduled six-rounder, while Big Boy went six-rounds to a draw with Lige Drew. Also in May, Big Boy beat Jimmy Lakes via a 4th-round TKO as Shorty (again rubbing salt into his brother's fresh wounds) beat Johnny Jackson twice, although the *San Diego Union* (May 18, 1940) had Jackson the winner in the first bout. On June 7, Shorty, in a rare failure, could not best his brother's effort against Lige Drew and also came away with a draw. It seems that 'Drew' lived up to his name when it came to his professional boxing career as he had 15 draws in 85 fights. On the same card, Big Boy, in his only outing for the month, met Aaron 'Al' Smith at the Hollywood Legion Stadium:

> "The contest was a mauling affair and furnished an upset. Smith, the short-ender, won over Hogue by a good margin. Big Boy started out like a winner and looked good for a few rounds, but, apparently not in condition, he blew up and could barely last the distance. In fact, Hogue collapsed immediately after the final gong sounded. Smith weighed 148, Hogue 152."

> —*THE RING,* September 1940

According to the *Nevada State Journal*:

"Hogue, exhausted after Smith's slashing body attack, collapsed in his corner after Referee Mushy Callahan raised Smith's hand in victory."

Neither of the twins appeared to be in fighting shape. The June 7 card in San Diego was the only time they both appeared together, but never won. Shorty followed up the draw with Drew with a 10-round decision over Honolulu-based Otto Blackwell (June 14) before knocking out Drew in a rematch (June 21).

In July 1940, Big Boy defeated Chuey Vargas for the third time, while Shorty won over Earl Stevenson and Rand Jackson (brother of Johnny). Shorty didn't fight in August, only the third time since starting out as a pro that he didn't see competition for an entire month. The reason for the boys being less active in the peak summer months was highlighted in the local press:

"HOGUES DROP MITTS FOR POLE SETTING

Jacumba. Aug. 27

Shorty and Big Boy Hogue dropped routine training today and accepted employment with a telephone crew which will reset poles in the vicinity of Mountain Springs grade.

A Highway 80 realignment project necessitates resetting the poles. The job will last about three months, it was said."

—*San Diego Union*, August 28, 1940

Although there was a good deal of regular manual work on the cards to keep the twins busy for the immediate future, they still kept up their boxing training for whatever ring action might come along. It was obvious that the twins' latest manager Tom Jones was looking to push both boys up the fistic ladder when he agreed to a match with former middleweight champion Fred Apostoli of San Francisco.

Known as 'The Fighting Bellhop,' Apostoli had learned to box in an orphanage in his early teens. He had been a professional fighter for six years by the time he took on Big Boy Hogue in San Francisco. In only his seventh fight, he was thrown in with the murderous-punching Freddie Steele of Tacoma, Washington and lasted into the tenth round before being stopped. He had also dropped points decisions to Ken Overlin, Young Corbett III and Billy Conn. On the plus side of the ledger, he had beaten Solly Krieger twice, had stopped middleweight champion Marcel Thil on a cut in an over-the-weight match in New York in 1937 and had gained revenge over Steele by stopping him in the 9th round of their January 1938 rematch in front of 10,000 at Madison Square Garden.

The high point of Apostoli's career came on November 18, 1938, when he won the New York version of the world middleweight title by stopping Young Corbett III in eight rounds. A kayo loss in seven rounds to Ceferino Garcia on October 2, 1939, ended Apostoli's title reign. Now, in his fourth bout since losing the title, Fred was looking to regain championship form with a victory over Big Boy:

"Freddie Apostoli of San Francisco takes on 19-year-old Willard "Big Boy" Hogue of San Diego tonight in a 10-round middleweight fight in which a defeat might mean Apostoli's goodbye to boxing.

A ring veteran at 26, Apostoli was conceded the edge on his 19-year-old opponent in weight, reach and experience. He knocked out Dale Sparr last month in five rounds.

Hogue's reputation, built in only one year of fighting, was expected to help fill the Coliseum Bowl in San Francisco."

—*Oakland Tribune,* August 19, 1940

At 27, Apostoli was far from washed-up, but there were some hard yards on his clock. Going into the Hogue fight, Apostoli, who just four months earlier had been written off by Nat Fleischer, was installed as a slight favorite:

"A loud laugh was the reply of veteran manager Tom Jones, who has handled three champs, to the 10 to 8 odds which favor Freddie Apostoli over "Big Boy" Hogue for their fight at Coliseum Bowl in San Francisco Monday night.

Jones saw Willard Hogue work out yesterday, and warned all and sundry not to sell the Southern boy short. In fact, Jones declared that Hogue will score an upset over the former champ, to definitely establish himself hereabouts.

Hogue has been making a fine impression in sparring sessions with his twin brother, "Shorty" Hogue, and is expected to prove a better opponent for Apostoli than Dale Sparr, who was kayoed in the fifth round."

—*Oakland Tribune,* August 18, 1940

"If Willard 'Big Boy' Hogue can display the same fighting ability in the ring as he has in his gymnasium workouts, San Francisco fight goers should see a donnybrook when he clashes with Fred Apostoli at the Coliseum Bowl this Monday night, August 19th.

Hogue, during his workouts, showed the railbirds an aggressive attack with both hands and good hitting power.

Apostoli, we all know, fights a good deal on the same order, so the fight figures to be one of those bruising affairs."

—*The Referee,* August 24, 1940

Apostoli held all of the aces as he had age, experience and weight on his side, but Big Boy was nothing if not game. Fred also claimed to be in the best shape of his life, thanks to his trainer Lew Powell. As it turned out, Apostoli's superior condition proved decisive since it was his aggressiveness in the closing rounds that allowed him to eke out a decision win:

"Willard 'Big Boy' Hogue of San Diego won the fans, if not the decision, in dropping a 10-round middleweight rough-and-tumble last night to San Francis-co's own Freddie Apostoli, who is on a comeback campaign.

The crowd was with the visitor almost to a man, as the 19-year-old Hogue fought gamely but futilely in the closing rounds against the former champion recognized in New York and California.

The youngster won four of the first five rounds, but Apostoli had squared things by the ninth and wound up with a bruising attack to the head. There were no knockdowns. Apostoli weighed 160, Hogue 157."

—*Oakland Tribune* August 20, 1940

According to the *San Francisco Chronicle:*

"This bout was filled with a lot of infighting. Hogue gave a good account of himself, but was battered by Apostoli in the last two rounds, as he was bleeding and exhausted."

THE *RING* magazine reported:

> "Willard (Big Boy) Hogue of the Jacumba, California Hogue twins, lost himself a 10-round decision to Fred Apostoli at the Coliseum Bowl, but he added a serious element of doubt to the possibility that the ex-bellhopper will ever again make the middleweight big time.
>
> Nothing more than a good club-fighter, Hogue stepped right along with Freddie for eight, bruising frames, only to fade badly in the ninth and tenth when he receipted for a two-handed shellacking that cost him the decision."

—*THE RING,* November, 1940

Following the Apostoli fight, Big Boy was approved to fight local boy Richard (Sheik) Rangel for a September 16 card in Fresno, California. However, there was a stipulation that he weigh-in at 150. According to the Fresno Bee (September 1, 1940) Big Boy withdrew due to a broken hand, so Georgie Crouch took his place. The injury kept him out of action until October 7. Meanwhile, when Shorty returned to action on September 27 after a couple of months off, to face Bert Velasquez in San Diego, he had gained 10 pounds and was looking puffy around the face. Even so, his lack of condition did not seem to affect his ring performance as he stopped Velasquez in the second round. Shorty then took on Billy Latka in San Francisco 10 days later, with Big Boy opposing Larry Derrick on the undercard. According to the press, Latka, who trained at Ryan's Gym under Joe Herman, was on a winning streak:

> "Shorty Hogue vs. Billy Latka, and Big Boy Hogue vs. Larry Derrick, middleweights are the two headlining bouts over the ten round route that are on tap for the fans at the Coliseum Bowl this Monday night, October 7th.

The Hogue boys are colorful fighters and promise the fans a good evening of entertainment. Latka has won his last eleven fights and seems to be well on his way. He is a good boxer and promises to make things interesting for 'Shorty'.

Derrick, Oakland negro, is a puncher. He holds kayo wins over Harry Cahill and Dick Foster. His bout with Big Boy should be loaded with action."

—*The Referee,* October 12, 1940

Since turning pro in March of 1938, Latka of San Jose, had compiled a record of 26 wins, three defeats and five draws. He had actually won nine of his previous 11 fights, which included a draw with Jimmy Casino (April 19) and a loss to Bobby Murphy.

According to Hal Tenney (THE RING, July 1940), Billy Latka was "built like an Adonis, looking like a Robert Taylor" in addition to being "exceptionally strong" and possessing "a knockout drop in either hand." Larry Derrick, a pro for over four years, had won 15 (nine by stoppage), had drawn one and lost seven — all on points:

"SAN FRANCISCO - Shorty Hogue won a ten-round decision over Billy Latka here last night in the main event at the Coliseum.

The San Diegan used his superior strength to carry the fight to Latka all the way. He hammered Latka steadily in close and, in the eighth round, dropped him for a count of two with a right to the jaw.

Latka's nose bled from the second round on. Latka, from San Jose, weighed 157-1/2 and Hogue 161.

Hogue's brother "Big Boy' was paired off in another ten rounder with Larry Derrick, Sacramento negro, but finished off his opponent by the technical knockout route in four rounds. The winner weighed 156 and Derrick 157-1/2."

—*Modesto Bee*, October, 8, 1940

Shorty came out of the win over Latka with a fractured hand and so concluded his second calendar year as a professional, his record now improved to 38–2-1 (won-lost-drawn).

A couple of weeks after stopping Larry Derrick, Big Boy traveled out of state for the first time as a professional. His opponent was local fighter and six-year veteran, Freddie Dixon. Originally from Bloomington, Illinois, Dixon started in the pro game at the age of 21, fighting in and around Peoria, Ill. Either there are bouts missing from his early record, or his management at the time were very brave or had total confidence in him. In his first six fights, Dixon's opponents had a combined record of 117-64-20. With 15 wins and a draw in his first 16 fights, Dixon had been touted as a hot prospect. His 17th opponent had been highly regarded veteran Izzy Jannazzo (at the time 28-16-11) to whom he lost a ten-round decision in Phoenix. Dixon then went on another streak, recording 13 wins and a draw, before dropping a decision to Kenny LaSalle.

By the time he stepped into the ring with Big Boy, Dixon was an established local favorite with 44 wins, three decision losses and five draws on his record. Nonetheless, Big Boy seemed to earn the favor of the local fans while winning a decision over the hometown boy:

"PHOENIX, Ariz., Oct. 25 (AP)— Big Boy Hogue of Jacumba, Calif., outpointed Freddie Dixon, Phoenix, to win a ten-round decision in the main event of a fight card last night.

The fight was stopped for several minutes in the sixth round when a number of fans, enraged at Dixon's butting tactics, invaded the ring. Hogue weighed 155 and Dixon 147-1/2."

—*Reno Evening Gazette,* October 25, 1940

November 1940 was the first month of the twins' pro career where neither of them saw any action. Shorty's ring record shows that the October fight against Billy Latka was his final contest for 1940, but according to Archie Moore (in his book *Any Boy Can: The Archie Moore Story*), he and Shorty met for the second time on December 5, 1940, at the San Diego Coliseum:

"My next fight was against a tough little scrapper by the name of Shorty Hogue in San Diego, and he decisioned me in a six-rounder on December 5,1940.

It was getting to be a habit with this guy, because he had outpointed me on December 21, 1939, before I left for Australia, but it was really no disgrace losing to him, as he was very good and one of my toughest opponents."

—Archie Moore

There was a show at the Coliseum that night, but it appears that neither the Hogue twins nor Archie Moore were on the five-bout card, and this second meeting with Shorty Hogue seems to be a phantom bout on the records of both fighters. Either way, Archie Moore was doing well enough at that stage of his career to be ranked the number four middleweight in the world.

Big Boy fought only once in December, and that was the result of circumstance rather than planning. In December each year, the *San Francisco Chronicle* staged a benefit card at the Coliseum Bowl. Matchmaker Benny Ford looked as though he had come up with a doozy for promoter Harry B. Smith (representing the *Chronicle*) when he signed local boy Pat Valentino to go against good English import Tommy Martin. Valentino was kayoed by a bout of flu, so Ford had to look elsewhere. His replacement looked equally exciting for the fans - Billy Soose versus Willard 'Big Boy' Hogue.

The matchmaker and the promoter probably felt like naughty boys being punished by Santa after Soose suffered some cracked ribs in a winning effort over Jimmy Casino on the 13th of the month. When Ford proposed Aaron (Little Tiger) Wade to replace Soose, it would have been perfectly acceptable for Big Boy to pull out as just about every middleweight on the Pacific Coast was steering clear of the Little Tiger.

Aaron Wade, one of three fighting brothers, was originally from Peoria, Illinois and had moved to San Francisco in order to further his boxing career. Some reports indicate that Wade had over 600 amateur bouts in and around his home town. While this seems like a fantastic amount of contests to have crammed into an estimated five-year career, he was good enough to be on the Chicago 'Inter-city' team with Tony Zale in 1935 and had been the first African-American to win a Peoria Golden Gloves title.

Although his earlier professional career may forever be shrouded by the mists of time, when he took the emergency call at Newman's Gym in San Francisco Wade already had a reputation as "a socker." The *Chronicle's* boxing beat reporter Eddie Muller had also described the Little Tiger as "a deadly puncher with both hands." Judging by reports of the action, Wade's reputation was deserved:

> "Aaron (Little Tiger) Wade of Peoria, Ill., forcing the fighting all the way, scored a technical knockout over Big Boy Hogue of San Diego in the ninth round of a Christmas charity ten rounder last night.
>
> Hogue suffered a badly cut eye in the eighth round and did not

answer the bell for the ninth. Wade weighed 152-1/2 and Hogue 158."

—*Fresno Bee,* December 21, 1940

The *Oakland Tribune* added:

"The Illinois negro was aggressive all the way and drew a good hand from the crowd of more than 4,000 which netted $3,400 gate."

The *Chronicle*'s Muller commented that the display by Wade was the best he had turned in to date. He also wrote: "Round after round the negro handed the tough Hogue a lacing. At times he hit him with left hooks and right crosses on the chin almost at will."

Wade had proven he was a level above the likes of Big Boy Hogue, and his record would attest to that fact. Later in his career, the 'Little Tiger' would break the ribs of one Sugar Ray Robinson in a street fight after Robinson wanted to cut Wade's sparring fees during the build up for Ray's December 1948 fight with Steve Belloise.

Big Boy finished his second calendar year in the pro ranks with a solid 38-5-5 tally. In the year-end ratings for THE RING, Archie Moore was placed high among the middleweights, and Turkey Thompson was making progress in the light-heavyweights, although he would soon balloon up in weight and end up competing in the top division.

Shorty squares up to Billy Latka (above) and Big Boy stands over Larry Derrick (photos courtesy of Mike Silver)

ROUND 5

Minneapolis: Friday January 9, 1942

"Although the fifth round went to Burley by a shade, it was still anybody's fight for Hogue was charging doggedly, swinging frequently and hard."

—Dick Cullum, *Minneapolis Daily Times*

CHAPTER SEVEN

B ig Boy came back after the 1940 holiday season to tackle Jimmy Casino (the breaker of Billy Soose's ribs) in San Diego. It was probably a little too soon after the beating that Wade had administered to him four weeks earlier as Casino knocked Big Boy out in under two rounds. A right to the jaw ended the matter at 1:36 of the second round. It was the first time that Big Boy had lost two fights back-to-back as a professional.

Benefiting from a couple of months off, Shorty started the year in fine form. He beat Charley Harris in five and Mac MacAbee in two (both in San Diego) before facing off for the second time against Archie Moore, his third fight in 28 days:

> "Followers of the fight game are not evenly divided. Moore is the favorite in the opinion of many experts. His loss to Hogue over a year ago is considered by those as *'one of those things.'* The negro was off form, had nothing to gain, and so on. Be all that past history as it may, there is one thing certain, Moore is out to win this time. He has to win. Hogue's victory is

one of the two black marks on Moore's record. If it is humanly possible for the St. Louis boy to win, he will do just that. He wants this one badly.

It has been said, and aptly that, *'Moore is a great fighter, Hogue is a good one.'* This may be the story behind the fight. Hogue looks inferior to Moore in workouts, it has been noted. This is perhaps true.

There have been champions, however, who looked foul in preps, but somehow, in a fight, they managed to hit and not get hit too much. By all the laws of observation, Moore's left hand should cut Hogue up in chunks, by the same token the youngster's infighting (a practice for which Moore has no affection) may jar the deadpan negro loose from his moorings to composure."

—*San Diego Tribune Sports,* January 31, 1941

Interestingly, the writer makes no mention of the December 5, 1940, meeting alluded to by Moore in his book *Any Boy Can*. The *San Diego Tribune*'s 'Tale of the Tape' for both combatants threw up some interesting numbers. Shorty had the advantage in weight - 162 to 159 - whilst Moore held a slight reach advantage – 74 inches vs 73 inches. Overall, Shorty appeared to be the more powerfully built of the two middleweights, with bigger calf, ankle, thigh, chest and neck measurements. According to the same stats, Archie, at 5 feet 11 inches, was the taller of the two by 1-1/2 inches. These figures may not be strictly accurate since military medical reports for Shorty actually list him as a quarter of an inch under 5 foot 8 inches.

Since their first meeting Moore had been busy amassing a seven-bout unbeaten streak in Australia, with knockouts over Jack McNamee, Atilio Sabatino, Joe Delaney, Frank Lindsay, Fred

Henneberry and Ron Richards (whom he also beat over ten rounds). A pair of 'welcome home' wins over Pancho Ramirez and Clay Rowan in San Diego took his unbeaten run to 11 straight. If Archie thought his Antipodean sojourn had left him ready to mix with the young wildcats of California, then he was sadly mistaken.

On Friday, 31 January, the Coliseum broke attendance records for its Friday night fights when over 4,000 rabid fans somehow squeezed into an area designed for 3,000; very few would be disappointed. Archie jabbed and moved his way to an early lead with Shorty boring in, searching for an opening of any kind. A solid body attack paved the way for similar success in the third, and the fourth round started in much the same way, with Moore jabbing and maneuvring and Shorty slamming in the hooks to the ribs and belly.

Just as Shorty appeared to be gaining an advantage, he walked straight into Moore's right hand which bounced him off the canvas. From that point forward, the war was on. Both threw caution to the winds at the outset of the fifth round, with Archie looking to press his advantage and Shorty trying to give him a taste of his own medicine. Moore's sharper punching gave him the edge until Shorty landed with a heavy barrage of shots just as the bell sounded.

Encouraged by his success at the end of the prior session, Shorty smelled blood, and he stormed out to meet Moore at the bell for the sixth. Archie caught Shorty early in the stanza, buckling his knees with a wicked right to the head. Sensing victory, Moore steamed in and plastered Shorty to head and body with shots that would have felled an ox. Falling back to the ropes, Shorty showed incredible heart, but could do little except evade the bombs coming at him from seemingly every direction. The bell eventually came to his rescue, bringing to conclusion a round which fans would talk about for a long time afterward.

Coming out for the seventh, there was a decided shift in the action. Moore, still exhausted from his efforts in the previous round, was slow getting started. Shorty, who had been on the wrong end of a murderous beating, showed the crowd what real heart and fitness were as he came back to take the next two rounds. In the ninth, Archie regained his composure and was again sharpshooting at the tank-like figure constantly pressuring him. Shorty was taking everything Moore dished out, and as the round drew to a close he returned fire with a barrage of shots that likely evened up the stanza.

The tenth started with Archie staggering Shorty once more, but the determined twin came back yet again to swamp Moore with a constant cascade of leather. The aggression, determination and sheer volume of punches was to be enough for referee Benny Whitman to cast his vote in favor of Shorty. The decision was a popular one as the crowd raised the roof with approval at the referee's call, though the consensus was that the reaction would have been the same had the call gone the other way. Afterward, promoter Benny Ford called the fight the greatest he had ever seen in a San Diego ring.

Moore took a month off before returning to meet the classy Eddie Booker, while Shorty, who didn't seem to know the meaning of the term 'rest', was back in action the following week on February 7 against one of the better middleweights on the coast at the time - Lloyd Marshall.

Born in Madison County, Georgia in 1914, Marshall was raised on a farm by his hard-working mother who had led an itinerant lifestyle, toiling in and around the southern states before finally settling in Cleveland. It was here that young Lloyd found boxing and proved to be an exceptional talent. It is reported that he lost only 17 of 200 bouts as an amateur. In two of his biggest bouts as a Simon Pure he was eliminated from the 1934 national championships at the semi-final stage by Fred Apostoli and was beaten in the 1935 final at middleweight by Dave Clark.

As an amateur, Lloyd passed up a chance to compete in the 1936 Olympic selection tournament. Wanting to contribute to the upkeep of the family, he instead turned to the punch-for-pay ranks with ex-fighter Johnny Papke as his manager. Marshall began in sterling fashion, and it was not long before the local pugs started to avoid him. A former outfielder for the Detroit Tigers by the name of Frank Doljack, suggested to Lloyd that he might do better for himself on the West Coast where Doljack himself just happened to be heading. Unfortunately, the fight game was not doing very well in Sacramento at the time. While Frank worked out with his new team, Marshall, struggling to survive with no income and no home, slept under the grandstand at the ballpark. Due to his baseball commitments, Doljack turned Lloyd over to local manager and promoter Jim Edwards.

Shorty was the underdog for the fight with Marshall, but the betting public was unaware of the hardships Lloyd had been forced to endure. Instead, they remembered the success he had enjoyed on the West Coast more than a year earlier when he won a ten-round victory over the more experienced Lou Brouillard at Oakland in December 1939. In the semi-final to Shorty's match-up with Marshall, Big Boy was matched with Paulie Watkins, and both twins had vowed to win for their ailing manager Tom Jones, who was confined to his hotel room on doctor's orders.

Shorty's performance against Marshall was an exhibition of what grit and determination can do for a fighter apparently out of his class skill-wise:

"Willis "Shorty" Hogue, 163-pound San Diego battler, scored an unexpected 10-round decision here last night over Lloyd Marshall, highly-touted Cleveland negro, 161-1/2, before a capacity house that required standing room ticket sales before the police ordered the doors closed.

Boring in continually, Hogue forced Marshall into a retreat after the third round and took six of the ten rounds with two even.

Willard 'Big Boy' Hogue, Shorty's twin, fought a six-round draw in the semi-windup with Polly Watkins, Marshall's stablemate. Big Boy weighed 162 and Watkins 159."

—Oakland Tribune, February 8, 1941

The *Sacramento Bee* (February 8) claimed that the event was the first sellout at the Memorial Auditorium in many a year. The following Monday (February 10), the *Fresno Bee* had this to say about attendance:

"Additional proof that the fight game is very much on the upgrade in California is the $3,500 gate Sacramento posted Friday night when Shorty Hogue beat Lloyd Marshall ... Fans still will turn out for what looks to them to be an even, honest to goodness match."

On February 26 Shorty knocked out Al Globe in three, and Big Boy won over eight rounds against Pancho Ramirez on a card in San Bernardino. Two weeks later, Big Boy was given the chance for revenge over Jimmy Casino in San Diego:

"*SAN DIEGO, March 8 - (AP)* - In a bruising, roughhouse battle that saw both fighters resort to butting and other unorthodox tactics, Big Boy Hogue, 157, Jacumba, mauled his way to a decision over Jimmy Casino, 162, Los Angeles, in a 10-round main event here last night."

—The Oakland Tribune, March 8, 1941

The next few months of their pro careers would be tough for Shorty and Big Boy. The talent pool on the West Coast was getting deeper, and both boys would soon be up to their necks in it. Shorty had proven his mettle against the wily Archie Moore and the dangerous Lloyd Marshall; come March 14, 1941, he would be tested further by the talented Eddie Booker of San Jose.

Originally from Alto, Texas, Hilton Edward Booker had an outstanding amateur career and carried that success over to the professional ranks, developing into a slick-boxing, defensive stylist under the tutelage of local trainer John Burdick. Unbeaten in his first 44 professional outings, Booker defeated Johnny Bassinelli, Remo Fernandez, Gail Harrington and the murderous-punching Jimmy Wakefield before dropping an eight-round decision to Pittsburgh veteran Fritzie Zivic at New York in 1939. This defeat was followed by another loss, this time over ten-rounds, to the veteran Cocoa Kid, the first and only time that Booker would lose back-to-back decisions. Taking most of 1940 off due to bad hands, Eddie had fought only four times since December 1939. His most recent successes had been wins over Chester Parks and Milo Theodorescu and a draw with Archie Moore in San Diego on February 26th.

The records of Hogue and Booker were similar, with Eddie's ledger containing 44 wins, two losses and five draws as compared with Shorty's 48 wins two losses and one draw. Both fighters had recorded extended unbeaten streaks, with Hogue having been undefeated in his last 30 fights and Booker having enjoyed separate runs of 41 and 11 fights without a loss sandwiched around his two defeats. Even their kayo records were similar, with Eddie boasting 22 stoppages and Shorty 19. One statistic, however, revealed an important difference between the two, namely that Booker had been fighting as a professional since January 1935 - a full four years longer than Shorty.

On the night of the fight, there was little to separate the two on the scales either, with Shorty coming in at 161 pounds and Booker at 160. Based on Shorty's previous performances, hopes were high for another slam-bang affair, and the action lived up to all expectations. Shorty was down in the fourth round and took a beating for the entire three minutes; other than that, the bout was a close one. The *San Diego Union* gave each fighter two rounds and scored six rounds even. The same reporter thought the bout belonged to Booker on the strength of his big fourth round, but the referee disagreed and declared the bout a draw. There were few complaints.

The California state rankings for the middleweight division (March, 1941) declared the title as vacant, and rated Eddie Booker as the leading contender with Shorty, Archie Moore, Little Tiger Wade and Jimmy Casino in hot pursuit. Big Boy didn't even figure in the welterweight rankings, which listed Jackie Wilson as the reigning champion.

Based on the action in the first fight, a rematch between Shorty and Booker seemed inevitable. Shorty had given everything he had in the first bout, and there were no expectations that the rematch would be any easier for either fighter. While Shorty decided to take it easy for a while, Booker stayed busy with a pair of ten-round wins in San Diego over Freddie Dixon and Leon Zorrita.

Meanwhile, Big Boy had agreed to take on the talented and under-appreciated, Allen Matthews in Seattle on April 22, 1941. The match would be only the second time Big Boy had fought outside of California as a pro. As it turned out, he might have been better off staying at home.

The veteran Matthews, once ranked among the top ten light-heavyweights in the world, was at the tail end of his career. A professional since 1929, he had fought the best in the world and had earned victories over most of them. Billy Rose, Benny Death-pane, Rosy Baker, Sammy Slaughter, Kid Leonard, Alabama Kid, Tommy Freeman, George Nichols, Freddie Steele, Al Host, Gus

Lesnevich, Fred Henneberry, Jack McNamee, Ken Overlin and Ceferino Garcia were part of an impressive parade of contenders and champions who had helped make Matthews the fighter he was. The truth was the St Louis legend was just too good for Big Boy, and he severely pasted him for most of the seven rounds of action:

> "Allen Matthews stopping Big Boy Hogue made the biggest splash in the local fistic circles. Allen's career may be largely behind him, but any of these rough, tough babies that bring the battle to him will wind up just where Mr. Hogue ended up. And that goes for your brother, too, Mr. Hogue."

—*THE RING*, July 1941

The Shorty Hogue vs Eddie Booker rematch was held at San Diego Coliseum on May 2, 1941 and was for the California state middleweight title. The belt had been in storage for seven years ever since Oscar Rankins had beaten Swede Berglund in 10 rounds at the Olympic Auditorium (October 1934).

The *Associated Press'* report of the Hogue vs Booker fight for the state title only gave Shorty (161-1/2) the eighth round. The second was tabbed as even, with Booker (156) winning the other eight rounds and the belt.

A month later, Shorty was involved in another rematch, this time against Lloyd Marshall. Once again the fight was contested in Marshall's adopted hometown of Sacramento. Their second meeting was no less entertaining than the first, with Marshall running off to an early lead after three rounds. Bloodied but unbowed, Shorty came back to take the next three stanzas. With the fight evenly balanced after six rounds, Marshall stepped on the gas and took the last four rounds. Referee Jack Downey gave the local boy the nod before the 4,000 in attendance. The defeat marked the first and only time that Shorty would lose consecutive decisions.

Lloyd Marshall would go on to have what can best be described as an up-and-down career. He would beat Ezzard Charles, Charley Burley, Anton Christoforidis, Curtis (Hatchetman) Sheppard, Joey Maxim, Freddie Mills, Jake LaMotta, Holman Williams and a host of other ranked fighters. However, he would lose in fights where he was the favorite:

"Lloyd Marshall to me was a bit of a riddle, too. He could be great, and then a let down in a later bout. You can best assess him by looking at his kayo of Charles, and the fact that he beat a few other world champions. I honestly could never figure out why he clung to boxing in Sacramento, where gate receipts had often been as low as $900 for some fights. I know he was sidestepped a lot by name fighters because of his punching power."

—Gabrielle 'Hap' Navarro

A cut sustained in the last round of the fight with Marshall, put Shorty out of action for a month. When he next stepped into the ring, August 1, 1941, for a fight with Ray Acosta he was not in the best of shape:

"Shorty Hogue has been holding his own with some of the country's best middleweights in recent months, but he was a big disappointment in his Hollywood debut.

Hogue won by a TKO in the 5th round over veteran Ray Acosta in the semi-windup to the Wilson-Cisneros go, but only after bringing down the wrath of the crowd for low punching.

However, Acosta feigned some of the pain, and when he bowed out it was more through discouragement than from injury. Shorty apparently wasn't in the best of condition, for he was Hogue (sic) fat, slow and tired easily."

—*THE RING*, October 1941

A newspaper report from June 24, 1941 provides probable cause for Shorty's apathetic approach to the Acosta fight. A broken nose, allegedly at the hands of his spouse, caused Shorty to file for divorce. He cited incidents of *"extreme cruelty"* against Virginia (Rigby) Hogue. The separation was not long in coming.

Shorty was in better shape the following week, when he beat Bobby Pacho over ten rounds in San Diego. Big Boy was featured on the same bill, stopping Charley Harris in four. The event marked the first time the twins had appeared on the same card since they both won in San Francisco ten months earlier.

For the next four weeks, the boys fought on alternate cards at the San Diego Coliseum. Big Boy defeated Freddie Dixon (again) on August 18, and the following week Shorty was back to his best as he ripped the state middleweight crown from the head of Eddie Booker:

"*SAN DIEGO, Aug. 22. (AP)*— Out-punching his opponent most of the way, Shorty Hogue, 158-1/2, Jacumba, took the California middleweight crown from Eddie Booker, 156-1/2, San Jose negro, in a rousing 10-round title bout here tonight.

Hogue, blocking cleverly and gaining a commanding margin in the infighting, had a clean-cut margin, winning six rounds. Booker won two, and two were even."

—*LA Times*, August 23, 1941

A tour of the Chicago area was arranged for the boys as they joined world heavyweight champion, Joe Louis, for his exhibition matches at the region's US Army camps. The twins played their part, showing in exhibition bouts in front of an estimated 10,000 military personnel at Camp Grant. On October 9, 1941, a recent recruit by the name of Bill Goertz took photographs of Joe Louis, his sparring/exhibition partner Selman Martins and the Hogue twins.

Back in San Diego the following week (October 12), a kayo win for Big Boy against Bernie Cardenas and a win for Shorty against Vern Earling (W10) set the boys up nicely for a return to the US Army training camp at Fort Custer, Michigan. Later in October, both boys were back in front of a paying crowd at Chicago Stadium. Shorty beat Johnny Barbara (TKO8) and Andre Jessurun (TKO7) in two promotions in the Windy City on October 24 and November 7, respectively. Big Boy appeared on the same cards, beating Mike Sopko (TKO5) and George Mitchell (KO8).

During their time in Chicago, Big Boy purchased a home movie camera, and footage shows the boys clowning around outside Eli's Ogden Huddle on the city's west side. The cafe had only been opened in 1940 by Eli M. Schulman, a former armed forces cook, who was keen on drumming up business. The twins, dressed in identical dark blue suits and white shirts topped off by heavy camel-colored overcoats, are seen standing outside the establishment pointing at a sign which reads: "If you are hungry and have no money, Come in We'll feed you for free." The boys enter the cafe and, after a scene change signifying the passage of time, are shown ambling back onto the street patting their stomachs, broad smiles of satisfaction on their faces.

On December 7, 1941, less than a month after the boys returned from Chicago, the Japanese air force bombed Pearl Harbor in Hawaii, leading the USA to declare war the next day on Japan and her allies. Despite the attack, some things carried on as normal, and on December 19, Shorty easily beat Young Gene Buffalo in front of a packed coliseum in San Diego. Big Boy lost on a second-round TKO to Bobby Birch of New York on the same bill.

Shorty had engaged in 15 contests that year; he had won 12 (seven knockouts), had lost two and drawn one. Big Boy had been in action 12 times for eight wins (five stoppages), with three losses and a draw. The December 19th event was particularly significant in that it marked the final, appearance of the Hogue twins together on the same bill.

One of the Hogue Twins

Camp Grant - ILL.

Big Boy (above) and Shorty (below) in just two of a number of photographs taken at Camp Grant by recruit, Bill Goertz. (Courtesy of Hans Ellund).

Other Hogue Twin

Camp Grant - ILL.

The twins boxing an exhibition for the troops at Camp Grant.
(Bill Goertz photo, courtesy of Hans Ellund)

Big Boy and Shorty in Chicago at the tail-end of 1941.
Image captured from home-movie footage provided by Hoby Hogue.

Lloyd Marshall (above) and Eddie Booker. Members of the infamous 'Murderers' Row' (Author's collection).

Jack Chase of Los Angeles via Denver, Colorado and Sherman, Texas.

Another member of the 'Murderers' Row.' (Author's collection)

Aaron 'Little Tiger' Wade of San Francisco via Peoria Ill.
(Author's collection)

ROUND 6

Minneapolis: Friday January 9, 1942

"It was not until the sixth that one man broke clearly into the lead, and that man was Burley.

A right to the jaw while Hogue was charging turned the tide. When Hogue staggered, Burley rushed to improve his advantage. Punching with beautiful smartness and accuracy, he dealt out terrific punishment before Hogue could settle down.

—Dick Cullum, *Minneapolis Daily Times*

Charley Burley of Pittsburgh. "Too good for his own good".
(Author's collection)

CHAPTER EIGHT

Shorty Hogue was in desperate trouble in his fight with Charley Burley at the Minneapolis Armory. Contested on even terms for the first five-and-a-bit rounds, Shorty was starting to feel the effects of the Pittsburgher's frequent and heavy bombardment. His left eye was closed, there was an inch-long gash on its eyebrow, the left side of his face was swollen to twice its normal size, there was a large swelling on his right cheekbone, his lips were puffed and cut, and his once reliable legs were struggling to keep him upright. With his opponent all-at-sea during rounds seven, eight and nine, Burley continued his sniping attack. Then, barely a minute into the tenth round, he moved in for the kill. A booming left hook cracked against Shorty's chin, sending him to the canvas for a count of six. He rose on unsteady legs only to be met with another left hook followed by a right hand — two punches thrown with such speed that the *Minneapolis Tribune*'s George A. Barton reported that they appeared to land simultaneously.

Shorty was so completely out, that referee Britt Gorman didn't even bother to count. Barton wrote that Burley " . . . turned in a masterful job of boxing, and accurate, punishing hitting. He jabbed and hooked Hogue dizzy with his rapier-like left hand and rocked him from head to heels with jolting rights."

Although he was unconscious for several minutes, Shorty recovered sufficiently in the dressing room to answer questions. Probably his most telling comment was the one reported the next day by Joe Hendrickson of the *Minneapolis Star*:

> *"'They say the punch you didn't see is the one that puts you away—Well, I don't recall seeing this one.'*
>
> In those few words, Shorty Hogue gives you a hint how skillfully Charley Burley knocked out the gallant curly head in the tenth round of their bruising battle at the Armory."

The knockout loss to Charley Burley was the only time Shorty didn't finish a fight conscious:

> "Recently, when Burley stopped Shorty Hogue, he did a brilliant job by scoring such a victory over a first class fighter.
>
> In 142 amateur and professional fights, Hogue had never been in serious trouble. It is always a tough problem to score a kayo for the first time over a smart, young boxer, yet Burley turned the trick. In accomplishing the feat, Burley showed a lot of smart fighting and boxing."

—*THE RING*, April 1942

Shorty was later quoted in the *San Diego Union* saying that Burley was not as good as Booker, Marshall or Moore. He also claimed that he was not right for the fight:

"I couldn't get started, and was in a rut from beginning to end. My usual style is to tear into my foe when he hits me. Instead, I just felt surprised that he had been able to get one over.

. . . when I meet him again, I'll knock him out."

—Shorty Hogue

Burley and his manager were delighted with the win, but were disappointed to learn that Hogue's California middleweight championship belt was not part of the spoils as California boxing rules state that a fighter has to be a resident of California in order to challenge for a title. As Shorty had indicated an interest in a rematch with Charley on the West Coast, the Burley team decided to relocate to San Diego and mount an official challenge for state honors:

"It's a caution the way that Charley Burley, the negro welterweight who recently took Shorty Hogue to the cleaners, manages to worm his way into the public print. Right now, Burley is forcing himself into the consciousness of San Diego fight fans by offering to come here to meet any opponent Promoter Linn Platner cares to select.

Hogue, who thinks he can take Burley the way Burley took him, would be a natural, but we are told that Manager Tom Jones isn't anxious to take the match until he can get Shorty in shape. In the meantime, Platner is buzzing the boxing camps in search of a suitable opponent, and right now has Milo Theodorescu in mind. If both are agreeable, Shorty's nemesis may show local fans how he did it."

—*San Diego Union,* January 30, 1942

Burley met Theodorescu at the San Diego Coliseum on February 6th and, in front of a packed house, Big Boy stepped into the ring to challenge the winner to a fight the following week.

> "One of the most efficient pieces of fighting machinery seen around these parts in some time, Burley simply ripped Theodorescu to pieces in the first three rounds, and referee John Perry stopped the slaughter in the fourth — out of sheer pity."

> —*San Diego Union,* February 7, 1942

Big Boy now had the opportunity to make amends for his brother's defeat. The papers and promoters built the fight into a grudge match, with the emphasis being on revenge for the Hogue family. Big Boy told the local press that the day of the bout, Friday the 13th, would be extremely unlucky for his opponent. Despite an advantage in the weight of around eight pounds, Big Boy was the underdog in the betting at 3-1 against, odds which proved to be justified:

> "Charley Burley scored a 'twin' victory when he flattened Big Boy Hogue in the sixth round at the San Diego Coliseum. Burley had already beaten the other Hogue twin, Shorty, at Minneapolis a few weeks previously. Although Hogue was completely out when the bout ended, Burley gets credit only for a TKO, as the gong ended the round with Big Boy flat on his back, unmindful of it all, having been put in that peaceful pose by a terrific right to the jaw. He was unable to answer the bell for the seventh.

> —*THE RING,* May 1942

"The lightning struck for the first time in the opening round when Burley brought Hogue's hands down with a couple of smashes to the ribs and then lashed out with a right which caught him flush on the jaw. Hogue went down for a count of nine, and then came up fighting. Burley waded in with both fists flying, and battered Hogue's face into a gory mess, but could not drop him again.

From that time on, Hogue absorbed terrific punishment, but never once gave ground. He continued to wade in with his hands over his face, trying to get in close for one finishing punch. Burley smashed away with both hands, alternating from body to head, but Hogue took it and fought back with every force at his command, even to the point of using his head with good effect in the clinches.

But as the fight wore on, and Burley continued to dish it out in generous doses, the only question at stake was how long it would last. Burley answered that by clipping the game Hogue with the finishing right late in the sixth."

—*San Diego Union,* February 14, 1942

It has been suggested by some, that the hard-punching Charley Burley ruined a lot of fighters. If you examine the careers of both Hogue boys following their losses to Burley, you can see how that argument might stand up in this instance. The Pittsburgh master boxer-puncher campaigned for several years, beating the likes of Jimmy Leto, Fritzie Zivic, Sonny Jones, Billy Soose, Holman Williams, Cocoa Kid, Aaron 'Tiger' Wade, Bert Lytell, Jack Chase, the Hogues, Nate Bolden, Joe Carter and Oakland Billy Smith. He also gave Archie Moore the boxing lesson of his life, knocking him down three time en route to a 10-round points win in Hollywood, April 1944:

"Charley Burley — pound for pound the greatest fighter I ever faced. Charley gave me a licking and sent me back to School. I learned more in our fight than in any other.

That man was fantastic; he could lean away from a punch, be clear off balance and knock your brains out with a counter."

—Archie Moore, *The Sunday Gleaner,* January 15, 1967

Sadly, Charley Burley never received the shot at the world championship he wanted or deserved as he was avoided by Henry Armstrong, Freddie Cochrane, Rocky Graziano and even the great Sugar Ray Robinson. He did, however, win the California middleweight title by knocking out Jack Chase in April 1944, and, in so doing, he earned the admiration of one of the state's most respected boxing historians:

"I have always believed that Charley Burley was the best middleweight I ever saw. The guy was a master. He could floor a vaunted opponent early on, and then seem to carry him the rest of the distance for whatever reason."

—Hap Navarro

Shorty recovered from his knockout loss to Burley enough to eke out a ten-round points win over Joe Sutka in Chicago around six weeks later (February 27, 1942), but the die was cast. Afterward, Shorty returned to San Diego to begin his dark descent into a world of shadows. It would be two months before he stepped into the ring again.

After his loss to Burley on February 13, Big Boy also took two months off, returning to action to defeat Billy Metcalf via a third-round kayo on April 10. A week later he upped the ante again, giving away 11 pounds to Johnny (Bandit) Romero in San Diego. The wily Mexican gave Big Boy a boxing lesson, out-thinking and out-punching him all the way. A cut over Big Boy's eye persuaded the referee Frankie Dolan of Los Angeles to call a halt after the ninth round. For his own return to the ring on April 24, Shorty fought 'Sailor' Jack Coggins at San Diego Coliseum:

> *"SAN DIEGO, April, 25—(AP).* Sailor Jack Coggins, former Pacific Fleet light-heavyweight champion, battered Shorty Hogue to the canvas twice last night before winning on a technical knockout in the ninth round of the Coliseum main event.
>
> Coggins floored the San Diego middleweight for a count of four in the first round, and again for an eight count in the ninth when referee Frank Holborow stopped the fight.
>
> Hogue, ranked sixth in national middleweight rankings entered the ring a heavy favorite over the big negro.
>
> Coggins, at 170, held a five pound weight advantage."

> —*The Modesto Bee,* April 25, 1942

There were a few more details about the stoppage reported in the *San Diego Union*:

> "In the first few seconds of the 9th round, Coggins scored with three left hooks, followed by a right hand that dropped Hogue hard. Hogue staggered to his feet and took two more punches, before the referee intervened."

A month later, in May 1942, Shorty experienced his final victory in the ring when he stopped Al Callahan in the fifth round. THE RING magazine reported that the Texan was outclassed from the start - hitting the canvas once in the third and three times in the fourth. It seemed that the only reason he lasted so long was because Shorty fought a slow and methodical battle.

It was becoming obvious that Shorty had slid backwards as he became easier to hit, hurt and bust up. Two weeks after the victory over Callaghan, he met Bobby Birch at San Diego in a ten-round main event:

"Bobby Birch, New York negro, put on a two-fisted attack in the seventh round of a scheduled ten against Shorty Hogue at the San Diego Coliseum, to win the bout by a T.K.O., due to cuts over both Hogue's eyes. Hogue butted Birch early in the seventh, the colored boxer became enraged, and the two slugged furiously until the end of the round. Bleeding from two deep cuts, Referee Joe Stone would not permit Hogue to continue in the eighth. Shorty had been floored for a count of six in the fourth."

—*THE RING*, September 1942

The eye damage put Shorty out of action for several weeks. In the meantime, Big Boy returned to action against Mexican southpaw Cecilio Lozada:

"Big Boy Hogue, 160, Jacumba, won a close decision over Cecilio Lozada, 151, Mexico, in a ten-rounder at the San Diego Coliseum.

The action was slow, but there was considerable punishment dealt out, as both tried for a knockout and landed some stiff punches.

Lozada was down in the second from a hard right to the body. The scrap was close enough to be called a draw without an injustice to either, but referee Barney Ross did not hesitate in raising Hogue's glove."

—*THE RING,* October 1942

Less than two weeks after the Lozada win, Big Boy was matched against newcomer Jack Chase in the main event at Snowy Baker's season opener at the Olympic Auditorium in Los Angeles. The brash Australian promoter was keen to reinvigorate the LA fight scene and had initiated new pricing policies, which included limiting reserved sections to only the first 12 rows on the floor and reducing prices drastically for the entire upstairs. Baker hoped that regular Tuesday night fights at 55 cents per seat in the upper sections (down from $3.30) would bring the crowds back to the Olympic.

Baker's initial six-bout card, the first at the venue in three months, was troubled from the outset as four of the featured fighters failed to appear and four of the card's six bouts ended early. If the new promoter feared the action was not competitive enough for those in attendance, however, he needn't have worried. The bout between Big Boy Hogue and Jack Chase was worth 55 cents of anyone's money.

In the days leading up to the event, *The Knockout* (July 25, 1942) ran a full-page advertisement which featured Big Boy photograph and a resume stating "The Hogue Twins are managed by John Dee Smith, 148 Broadway, San Diego, Calif." The publication also said of the match:

"Hogue is a wicked body belter and will chase Jack from start to finish. Jack is hard to catch up with tho. Should be a real fight all the way. If Big Boy stays in close and hammers at Jack's body he can win."

Unfortunately for Big Boy, "staying close" was not a part of Chase's strategy the night of the fight:

> "Chase packed too much long-range artillery for Hogue, a rough, tough customer who never quit trying but lacked the natural ability of the rangy negro.
>
> Chase had Hogue on the deck for the count of nine from a right to the chin in the third round, and in the waning stages of the bout landed so many Sunday rights on Hogue's left eye that he finally opened up a nasty cut in the last heat.
>
> Hogue, at a tremendous disadvantage in reach, kept boring in but was forced to take one stabbing left to the face after another in order to gain an opening."

—Paul Lowry, The *LA Times*, July 22, 1942

THE RING (October, 1942) stated: "Big Boy was the recipient of flocks of left jabs."

Jack (James Isaiah) Chase, a Texan by birth, had developed into a solid professional in the mountain region surrounding Walsenburg, Colorado. Brought up without a father, Chase was constantly in trouble as a youth and had spent a sizable portion of his younger days in the equivalent of juvenile hall. While most sources list 1936 as his first year in the fight game, recent research has uncovered as yet unsubstantiated information that he may have had in excess of 30 fights during the years prior to knocking out Mike Montoya in six rounds for the state title (Walsenburg, Colorado 1936). If 1936 was indeed his first year in the ring, Chase got off to a good start, having lost only four of a reported 34 fights between 1936 and 1937.

His promising pro career stalled when he was found guilty of almost beating a guard to death with a lead pipe during a botched robbery. After more than two years in Colorado's Canon City prison, he continued where he left off in the boxing game, but bad luck seemed to follow him.

On August 31, 1941, he fought Roy (Jack) Gillespie in Denver. Gillespie was knocked out and died of his injuries three days later. Chase, who up until then fought as 'Young Joe Louis', fought only once more in Colorado, a twelve-round draw with Billy Prior. He then moved to California and changed his name to 'Jack' Chase, perhaps reinventing himself in order to make a new start.

Prior to the fight with Big Boy Hogue, Chase had fought nine times on the Coast. He had won six decision bouts, scored one KO and had two draws. Following the win over Big Boy, Chase went on to beat Bobby Birch twice in back-to-back fights in Los Angeles, thus cementing his growing reputation as a force to be reckoned with in California:

"Chase was something else. A classic boxer par-excellence who did everything by the book. If you know about his early days in the game, you are aware of his enormous string of wins as Young Joe Louis.

When I knew Jack or saw him last he was training and schooling Art Aragon around 1949 for manager Jimmy Roche."

—Hap Navarro

Three days after Big Boy's loss to Chase, Shorty had an opportunity to maintain his record of beating every man he had ever faced when he squared off for a second time with Bobby Birch:

"Bobby Birch, New York negro, made his second victory over

131

Shorty Hogue a more decisive and destructive one than his first over the Jacumba twin.

This return ten-rounder, also at the San Diego Coliseum, was a close, vicious scrap for the first two rounds, both boys receiving much punishment. But Birch came out like a tiger in the third and punched Shorty all over the place.

The twin barely made his stool at the end of the round. With his nose battered, his handlers requested referee Holborow to call it a day, which gave the New Yorker a third-round T.K.O. victory. Birch weighed 158, Hogue 163."

—*THE RING,* October 1942

"Hogue was doing well for the first round and a half, until he missed with a left hook and was countered and hurt by Birch with a right hand.

Hogue took a pounding in the 3rd round, as he was sent twice sagging into the ropes and went back to his corner unsteady with a broken nose as the round ended. Hogue's corner and the referee decided to stop the bout."

—*San Diego Union,* July 22, 1942

Bobby Birch holds the distinction of being the only fighter Shorty Hogue could not beat, when given more than one opportunity to do so. Previously, anyone Shorty lost to always got pegged back in a second or third meeting, not so with Birch. The New Yorker had the hex sign over the Hogue twins, but he could not get the same result over many of the division's other top men. Bobby, who fought from 1937 to 1947, lost to Ken Overlin, Harvey Massey (twice), Jack Chase (twice), Aaron Wade, Charley Burley and Eddie Booker (in a challenge for the California state middleweight title). To his credit, Birch went the distance with all of them.

The damage to Shorty's nose must not have been too bad since he was back in the ring just three weeks later (August 14, 1942) for what would be his fourth and final encounter with Eddie Booker. Shorty was still California state middleweight champion, and the agreement was that the title was on the line for the main event at the San Diego Coliseum. Since their last meeting 12 months earlier, Booker had engaged in only three fights - a three-round KO of Billy Connerty in Montana, a ten-round draw with Johnny Romero in San Diego and a points win over ten against Castillo Cruz in Oakland. In view of his reduced level of activity, it would have been no surprise if Booker had shown a few signs of ring rust - but if he did, it wasn't obvious:

> "Eddie Booker, classy negro boxer of San Jose, won the California middleweight title by stopping Shorty Hogue of Jacumba in eight rounds at the San Diego Coliseum.
>
> Booker performed like a man who could just have well have been fighting for a world's title instead of a state crown.
>
> The colored sharp-shooter won every round. He had Hogue in a groggy condition in the seventh and opened old cuts over both Shorty's eyes in the eighth.
>
> Referee Benny Whitman considered Hogue in no condition to continue in the ninth and awarded the bout to Booker on a T.K.O. It had been scheduled for twelve rounds. Each weighed 160."
>
> —*THE RING*, November 1942

> "Booker won every round, as he kept Hogue in a shell for most of the fight.

One of Hogue's eyes eventually swelled shut and cut, which led his corner to stop the fight between the 8th and 9th rounds.

Hogue was staggered in the 6th round, with the bell saving him before Booker could follow up."

—*San Diego Union*, August 15, 1942

The *Fresno Bee* (August 15, 1942) reported that Shorty's eye had been closed in the early rounds and was then *"severely cut"* prior to his seconds throwing in the towel at the end of the eighth round.

Just ten days after regaining the state title from Shorty, Booker beat former welterweight championship contender Izzy Jannazzo over ten rounds in San Francisco. He then defended his California crown by winning a 12-round decision over Bobby Birch on September 4 in the Hogues' own backyard.

On September 11, 1942 Shorty again tangled with Johnny Romero - this time conceding substantial poundage to the Bandit:

"SAN DIEGO, Calif., Sept. 12. (UP)—Johnny Romero gave Willis (Shorty) Hogue a sad send-off into the Navy by handing a TKO at the end of the sixth round of a scheduled 10 round bout here last night. Hogue, who hails from Jacumba, Calif., dons navy blues Monday. Romero, from San Diego, tipped the scales at 178; Hogue at 169."

—*Nevada State Journal*, September 13, 1942

"It was a slow, uninteresting affair. Hogue looked bad. Shorty has slipped greatly in recent months. He remains in a shell most of the time, rarely leading, and when he did punch, his heavy-hitting ability was missing.

Romero showed little inclination to fight during the first four rounds, but in the fifth the Bandit opened up and so did Hogue's old eye wounds. Shorty's cuts were more aggravated in the sixth and he failed to answer the gong for the seventh."

—*THE RING*, December 1942

According to the *Oakland Tribune* (September 19, 1942) Romero vs Shorty drew around $2,500; the crowds and the paydays were dwindling.

On September 15, when his face would still be displaying evidence of the beating Bandit Romero administered to him four days earlier, Shorty signed up for two years as an apprentice seaman. He was supported in this endeavor by Big Boy who signed as a witness on Shorty's ID papers.

By this time, Shorty had divorced Virginia and had married one Barbara Joan Melonas. Both the navy life and the third marriage would prove to be extremely short-lived.

Three days after Shorty's enlistment, on September 18, Big Boy took on Eddie Booker in another fruitless attempt to gain revenge for the Hogue family. The only thing Big Boy came out of the fight with was confirmation that he was probably not as good as his brother:

"Eddie Booker, San Jose negro, retained his state middleweight title without working up a sweat when his bout with Big Boy Hogue at the San Diego Coliseum was halted at the end of the third round. Hogue received a cut over his left eye that the club physician considered too serious for the twin to continue.

Big Boy had been wading in and had landed some stiff punches occasionally, but he was no match for Booker's clever boxing and was on the receiving end of a shellacking most of the time.

Each of these Hogue twins always insists on meeting the conqueror of his brother, even though he is really no match for the fighter who did defeat the other twin. Booker had won the state title from Shorty Hogue, who is considered a better fighter than Big Boy."

—*THE RING*, December 1942

Going on to record a win against Lloyd Marshall and a draw with Archie Moore, Booker would remain unbeaten for the remainder of 1942. He would lose only once in his remaining eight fights before retiring due to eye problems in 1944.

Shorty Hogue had engaged in eight fights for the year; six less than in 1941. He had won only two and had lost six times via the short route. The six losses in eight fights were more defeats than he had suffered in the previous three years and 58 fights.

Big Boy had fought even less, with two wins and five losses from seven fights. The twins' common opponents had been Charley Burley (lost TKO 10 and lost TKO 7), Eddie Booker (lost TKO 8 and lost TKO 4) and Johnny Romero (lost TKO 7 and lost TKO 9). Both Shorty and Big Boy had each fought some 400 rounds in a little over three years of professional competition.

As a comparison, Marvelous Marvin Hagler - the middleweight champion of the world from 1980 to 1987 - fought 398 rounds in a 67-fight, 14-year career. Another point of reference is the career of Tony Zale, world champion when Shorty was contending for the middleweight title, who logged in a total of 501 rounds in 87 contests from 1934 to 1948. Even if one discounts the four years during which Zale's title was frozen due to WWII (February 1942 to January 1946), Tony still fought an average of only 50 rounds per year — and Hagler an average of 28. The Hogue twins, on the other hand, racked up well in excess of 100 rounds per year (a 133 per-year average).

Given the undeniable savagery of the bouts in which they engaged, it is little wonder they burned out so early.

CHAPTER NINE

A week after enlisting, Shorty was transferred to Naval Training School (NTS) San Diego to commence training. Between October 1 and October 15, he was put through his paces before being shipped out to US Naval Air Station San Diego for duty.

Big Boy carried on in the fight game and, on October 2nd, he lost on points over ten rounds to Billy Beauhuld in San Diego. 'Irish' Billy was a tough customer as evidenced by his subsequent participation in the war effort in the Pacific. In a March 9, 1943 interview with a reporter from the *Telegram Tribune* (San Luis Obispo), he recounted a time at Guadalcanal when he was almost killed in action during a patrol for Japanese troops on January 31, 1943:

"We were following a stream up the island. We came on them pretty soon, all sleeping in fox holes. I began advancing toward the fox hole I had been assigned, and I could hear shots ringing out as the other boys closed-in. The shooting woke up my opponent.

He popped out of that fox hole and looked me straight in the face from 10 feet away. Then he picked up a Luger .38 pistol and fired it at me. The bullet hit me in the hand, ripping my middle finger. It made me drop my rifle, and there I stood.

I jumped for the fox hole, jerking out the six dollar knife I had bought in San Diego. The Jap shot again, and this time he hit me in the knee, but I was moving forward and I plumped down on him. I got that knife going, and that was all for Mr Jap."

Beauhuld, (born William Madden in St Louis in 1916), fought predominantly on the East Coast, amassing a 55-14-9 record before running into the less well-armed Big Boy Hogue. Billy's win over Big Boy was his last before entering the military. After the war, he had only one more fight — a TKO loss to Max Hutchins at the Coliseum.

Big Boy made the local press a couple of weeks after the Beauhuld loss when he was arrested for his part in a robbery. An October 17 report in the *San Diego Union* stated that Big Boy and one Homer Evans (38) had been charged with taking $180 from a Franklin J. Cadwell of El Cajon. Both offenders were held in the county jail under $1,000 bond. The victim claimed that Hogue and Franklin were at his home playing poker when a fight broke out. Cadwell told police that he was beaten before being robbed by the pair.

Big Boy was signed to meet Archie Moore in the main event at the Coliseum in San Diego on October 30, 1942. The robbery charge hanging over him undoubtedly affected his preparations, yet he still held public workouts at 1 p.m. each day during the build-up to the fight. The day before the Moore bout, the charges were dismissed by Municipal Judge A. F. Molina, on motion of the district attorney. It was discovered that the victim had cheated during the game and that the accused had only taken back the money he had 'won' from them.

The next day, Big Boy was crossing the street when he had an alter-cation with the ripped and rusted fender of a parked car. His leg was so badly gashed he was not to meet Moore that night, so a call was put out for a stand-in, and someone had the bright idea that Shorty should replace his brother.

Having previously been on the losing end of decisions to Shorty, Moore jumped at the chance for revenge. Based on the next day's news accounts, the bout was little more than a light workout for Archie, as Shorty was unable to offer anything other than token resistance. Down twice in the first round, Shorty was buffeted around the ring in the second until he fell defenseless into the ropes. Referee Joe Stone called a halt to the shambles, and to Shorty's career as a fighter, part way through the round.

Shorty returned to the naval base to continue his national service, but it soon became apparent all was not well. Shorty's nephew, Bob Dye, said that in early-to-mid 1942 Shorty's behavior had become very strange:

> "That was the time (1942) Shorty was showing signs of mental problems. We were in a cafe once in Porterville, and I set a glass that was left earlier by folks on the table. I set it on another table, and Shorty said *'Mark told me you would set that there.'* And many times he would say Mark told him to do that. And no one knew who Mark was."
>
> —Bob Dye

A document in Shorty's service records states that on November 16, 1942, he was "transferred this date to US Naval Hospital, San Diego, California for medical treatment." The same record goes on: "Transferred in accordance with article D-7017 Bunac Manual 1925. ... Hospitalized for disability not result of own misconduct." Shorty remained in hospital until November 25, at which time he returned to normal service.

Even though his naval service eventually would force Shorty to accept the fact that his boxing days ended in 1942, the top-ten ratings at the time were still loaded with men against whom he had recently competed. The RING rankings at year's end listed Archie Moore, Charley Burley, Jack Chase, and Eddie Booker last first, second, seventh, and eighth middleweight contenders, respectively, while among the light heavyweights, Lloyd Marshall, Jack Coggins, and Johnny (Bandit) Romero were ranked as the fifth, sixth, and ninth leading contenders.

Clearly the Shorty Hogue express had derailed and been forced to come to a sudden and unexpected halt. Shorty had rated as a top contender at the start of 1942, but the crushing loss to Burley set into motion a horrendous nine-bout run which left him with a record of only two wins and seven kayo defeats for the year. Taking into account the fact that Shorty was essentially a blown-up welterweight, one thing stands out. He had been mixing with a great deal of naturally bigger fighters — and not many of them could be classified as 'soft-touches.'

The transition from San Diego 'boxing celebrity' to navy grunt could not have been easy on Shorty, either. He spent the first couple of months away from boxing struggling with his sense of place and purpose, and it is likely that his deteriorating mental condition did not help matters. His new-found 'friend' - Mark - also appeared to be a constant companion. Family members heard plenty about what Mark had to say, but had no idea who Mark was because they never met him. No one but Shorty ever saw or heard him either as he existed in Shorty's mind only.

On the evening of January 14, 1943, Shorty had been on a night out at the Coliseum. Shortly after 9.00 p.m., after drinking a couple of shots of whiskey and two five-cent glasses of beer, he got into his car and left for home. Heading west along Broadway, he then turned right onto Park Boulevard. As he headed north past C Street, a San Diego Police patrol car was traveling east on Russ Street, also heading toward Park Boulevard. Shorty drove across B Street and then across Russ, where the police officers spotted him. They turned left onto Park Boulevard and followed Shorty as far as the corner of Laurel and Park, where they pulled him over. Shorty was initially confused as to why he had been stopped:

"When I was half way home, I heard a siren. Right away, I looked down at my speedometer. I thought I might have been going too fast for dim-out, but I was going close to 23 miles an hour. I was wondering what in the world was the matter. I found out right away."

—Statement of HOGUE, Willis Burton, Sea2c., W Division

In their own statements contained within Shorty's service records, San Diego Police Officers Biddle and Davis gave their reason for pulling him over:

"Cruising North on Park Blvd from Russ, we saw a Pont 1940 coupe, license 5OA768, being driven north on Park Blvd, this car was traveling at app 25 to 35 MPH varying — being driven with very bright lights, (high beam), this car covering much of the roadway, many times crossing over the center white line. We stopped this car at Laurel and Park Blvd. in the car, along, we found the defendant, driving same."

Shorty's version of the events are also recorded in his military personnel file:

"The cops spoke gruff like and said, *'What's the matter fellow, don't you know this is blackout time?'* then I knew what was the matter. I was driving with my bright lights on. I had just gotten my car fixed for dim-out and my mind being elsewhere, I forgot to dim my lights. On this same day I was arrested, I had fixed three ping pong tables so that the fellows could play ping pong. It made me feel good to know that I had pleased them. I had been thinking about that so much while driving I just wasn't thinking about my lights, and I was hoping to please my lieutenant, for he is a swell fellow. My wife had put my driver's license on the steering post in the car and I had forgotten that it was there."

—*Statement of HOGUE, Willis Burton, Sea2c., W Division*

The official statements of officers Biddle and Davis record what happened next:

"He smelled strongly of whiskey, we asked him to get out of the car, and when asked to stand and talk to us, he almost fell over, he was very much under the influence of the drinks and admitted having. He had no driver license in his possession and stated that he didn't know if he had one or not, stated he used to have one. He was arrested. The Pont Coupe was impounded for safe keeping."

Shorty was charged with violation. of California Vehicle Code (CVC) 502 (drunk driving), CVC 250A (no driver's license) and of San Diego City Traffic Ordinance #2560 (violation of dim-out) and was held overnight. According to log notes, the Chief Petty Officer on watch observed that the offender displayed: "Breath alcoholic, speech clear, gait unsteady, uniform dirty." He was released at 10.10 a.m. the next morning and sent back to work.

Shorty faced no penalty for his indiscretion as on January 16, 1943, Lieutenant G. H. Gregory filed a report to a Commander Lowry stating; "This man, an ex-fighter, is honestly punch drunk, and totally unsuited for the Navy. I believe he should be given an Inaptitude Discharge immediately."

Shorty then underwent further assessment and examination, and by January 21ˢᵗ the verdict was in. Eight days later, Shorty signed an affidavit stating that the medical condition existed prior to his enlistment and had not been exacerbated by service conditions. The final medical report makes for sober reading:

"FACTS ARE AS FOLLOWS: This twenty-two year old seaman, Second Class, US Naval Reserve, has had four months and six days service prior to his admission to the sick list at the US Naval Air Station, San Diego, California, because of depression and inability to do his work. The general physical, neurological, special and laboratory examinations, including spinal fluid, have been normal except for a positive Chaddock, absent abdominal reflexes, accentuated knee jerks, and a positive Romberg. An X-ray examination of the skull was negative.

According to the man's own statement, accepted by the board, he did poorly in school, leaving at the end of three years of high school, in order to devote his time to professional boxing. He has boxed since the age of fifteen, and has been technically knocked out six times. About a year ago, he became depressed following the cancellation of a boxing match at the declaration of war. He has had several automobile accidents, admittedly due to his negligence, indifference and carelessness.

The neurophysiological findings are those of diffuse, chronic, organic, degenerative cerebral changes with apathy and indifference in a professional boxer who has had repeated head trauma. He exhibits memory defects, inability to comprehend anything more than a simple problem and reveals poor judgment. There has been no evidence of psychosis.

Since admission, he is adjusting to his pre-enlistment social and emotional level.

The patient's statement of acquiescence is appended. Maximum benefit from hospitalization has been attained."

The official diagnosis by the Naval medical staff was "traumatic encephalopathy."

Shorty would undergo further medical evaluation and would stay out of trouble until March 5, 1943, when he went AWOL at 11.00 p.m. and remained absent until 11.30 a.m. on March 9, when he returned to base. He was then sent back to the naval hospital and a final medical report, of March 16, resulted in an 'Honorable Discharge' from the Naval Reserve.

Come April 9, 1943, Shorty Hogue — former amateur boxing champion, state champion and world-ranked fighter — was now also ex-naval reserve. He was provided with a travel allowance for the bus back to San Diego town centre and ejected from the Navy. Mentally unfit for military service, physically no longer able to continue in his chosen profession, and with no discernible skills, he was consigned to the scrap heap at 22.

While Shorty was still undergoing medical assessments, Big Boy TKO'd Dick Richie in eight rounds on March 19, 1943, in a fight that was to be his last win. While the twins were drifting out of contender status, their former manager Tom Jones remained active in boxing circles and was looking at any and all angles for promotional or managerial opportunities:

"LOS ANGELES—Jack Johnson, who lifted the world's heavyweight title from Jim Jeffries in 1910, was granted permission by the California Athletic Commission to box

exhibition matches, provided he can pass a physical examination.

The big negro, now 64 years old, said he was confident of his physical fitness, but the commission specified that Jack's bouts would be no more than three rounds of two minutes each against approved opponents. Tom Jones, former manager of Ad Wolgast, Billy Papke, Jess Willard and others, will book Johnson for these exhibitions.

Johnson was also granted a guest referee's license."

—Hayward Review, March 9, 1943

The fact that the former heavyweight champion of the world could be passed fit to box exhibitions at the age of 65 is an illustration of how the boxing world was getting along just fine without Shorty Hogue. By May 1943, Shorty and Big Boy were spending an increasing amount of time in Reno, Nevada with their brother Nip, who operated the '21' game at the 116 Casino. Nip was involved with a few unsavory characters in Reno, none more despicable it seems, than a fellow by the name of Clifford Judd.

Judd (born in June, 1913) was 30 years old when he first got to know the twins. Together, he and Nip introduced Shorty and Big Boy to gambling, card cheating and drugs. Big Boy took to gambling and card cheating like the proverbial duck to water. According to Tom Brady (a friend of the twins' nephew Richard Plummer), Big Boy showed Richard and Tom how to cheat at cards. Big Boy also told them that they couldn't use any of it in Vegas, but he knew of lots of private games in Reno where they could make big bucks. Tom said they both turned him down. He also said you couldn't trust Big Boy, but that Shorty was the nicest guy you could meet.

Shorty lingered in Reno for much of May, assisting Nip with his '21' table. By July, Big Boy was back in action as he had signed to fight

Eddie Booker at Lane Field. He might have been better off staying in Reno.

The fight ran into a hitch when the local commission refused to authorise the match due to Booker's failing sight in one eye. To compensate for the loss of such an important attraction, the promoter installed Archie Moore as a substitute for Booker.

"SAN DIEGO, Cal., July 22. (UP)—Archie Moore, one of the nation's top middleweights, tonight took a five round TKO from Big Boy Hogue, San Diego boxer who is trying a comeback.

Moore, whose contract was recently bought by fighter Henry Armstrong, and who begins a tour of the east next month, had little trouble in polishing off the San Diego twin and had him groggy when the referee stopped the bout. Both lads weighed in at 160 each."

—*Nevada State Journal Sports*, July 23, 1943

"SAN DIEGO, Cal., July 22. (UP) — Archie Moore, California middleweight champion and Big Boy Hogue of Jacumba, had each other on the canvas in their non-title bout last night, but Moore had his opponent in such a bad way later that referee Lee Ramage halted the bout in the fifth round and awarded the champ the technical knockout. The bout was a scheduled 10 rounder.

More than 4,000 attended the first outdoor, night boxing card here since Pearl Harbor."

—*Modesto Bee*, July 23, 1943

Eight weeks later, Big Boy signed up for another fight, this time with Moore's training partner, Tom 'Kid' Lester. Shorty, who was recently divorced from Barbara Melonas, was in no physical condition to be in the ring, yet he assisted his brother in preparations; a draw over 10 rounds was the best Big Boy could muster:

"Big Boy Hogue, 157, and Kid Lester, 156, battled to a ten round draw at the San Diego Coliseum. Both came out at the opening bell with intent (sic) of scoring a quick knockout and Lester came close to accomplishing it.

The negro landed hard in the first few seconds of the bout and had Hogue in a bad way and the Kid gave the twin a terrible lacing all during the first heat in his efforts to finish him, but Hogue survived the round.

Lester won the next two frames, but the twin continued to regain strength, while the colored toughie was playing out from his efforts, and in the fourth, Big Boy started to dish it out to the Kid. With the fray even going into the final round, both went all out to grab the advantage, but it ended up in a dead heat."

—*THE RING*, December 1943

The following week, Big Boy fought Billy Morris over the same distance, but didn't fare any better:

"Bill Morris, 149, Pittsburgh negro, decisioned Big Boy Hogue, 157, Jacumba, in ten tough rounds at the San Diego Coliseum.

Hogue went down for a no-count in the first round from a stiff left. Morris also won the second heat, but Big Boy put on a blitzkrieg in the third to shake up and bloody the colored boxer.

The twin also grabbed the fourth and fifth frames, but by close margins.

Morris changed his tactics in the sixth, resorting to back-pedalling and counter-punching, and this style of boxing kept him out in front in the next three rounds. Although Hogue forced the milling all the way and rocked Billy on numerous occasions, the Pittsburgher had a slight lead going into the tenth, and he widened the gap by going into high (gear) and dishing out a lacing to the twin in the final round."

—*THE RING,* December 1943

After taking five weeks off, Big Boy fought again in San Diego, this time to a no contest against Battling Monroe. He then signed up to fight Rusty Payne:

"It is a case of 'When a feller needs a friend' with Big Boy Hogue of Jacumba. The twin insists on fighting guys that he cannot whip, and he is taking some bad beatings because of his poor judgment.

After being held to a draw by the smaller and less talented Kid Lester, Hogue comes right back against bigger and better Rusty Payne.

Result: 'stpd. by in 1'.

Hogue came out at the opening gong flailing both fists. Payne jabbed him off, sank a left into the twin's stomach, and dropped him for a count of nine with terrific right to the jaw.

Hogue arose groggily and Rusty knocked him into the ropes with another solid right to the head and moved in to finish his defenceless foe, but referee Joe Stone, using good judgement, stepped between them and raised the negro's hand.

Time, 1:20.

Payne weighed 174; Hogue, 162."

THE RING, March 1944

Big Boy's recent run of results — a points loss (Billy Morris), a draw (Kid Lester), a No Contest bout (Battling Monroe) and two TKO losses (Archie Moore and Rusty Payne) were evidence of his continuing backward slide. On December 28, 1943, the state commission suspended him from further activity due to "lack of condition."

The younger twins had outlasted his brother in the ring by just over a year. Shorty ended his four-year professional career with a tally of 52 (24 by KO)–11–2. Big Boy ended with a record of 49 (18 by KO)–17–7 with one 'no-contest.' That really should have been the end for both of them as far as professional fighters, but as we all know, the fighters themselves are usually the last to admit when it is time to hang up the gloves.

Shorty's medical diagnosis in itself should have been enough to convince him that his time in the ring was up. The 'official' word on his honorable discharge from the Navy was that it was for 'Durocher Ear' — or a perforated eardrum — and Shorty probably kidded himself that he was fit to continue. Having a friend like Cliff Judd couldn't have helped his decision-making either.

Barely six months after the death of his old manager Tom Jones at age 69 (January 9, 1944), Shorty was looking to make a comeback. By May 1944, he had signed up with Cliff Judd as his manager and was back training and sparring:

"Encouraged by Cliff Judd, local sportsman who has assumed his managerial chores, Shorty has been training faithfully. Judd, former star Oregon high school athlete, has been sparring daily with the middleweight and they've gone as many as eight rounds daily at the 'Y' gym."

—*Nevada State Journal,* May 17, 1944

Moving around the ring with someone with limited experience of competitive fighting is hardly sound preparation for the real thing. Fortunately, Shorty was able to get in some training rounds with a fighter of proven pedigree and class, Holman Williams. The Detroit marvel — at the time a veteran of almost 150 recorded bouts — was preparing for a fight on June 7 against Lloyd Marshall in Oakland, California. Williams' manager, 'Broadway' Charley Rose, saw Shorty in action against Williams, and he predicted Shorty would be successful in his comeback. Cliff Judd must have believed it too, as he attempted to set his charge a very challenging route back to the spotlight.

The *Nevada State Journal* (May 24, 1944), reported that Judd had lined up a bout for Shorty on June 6 in Sacramento. His opponent was to be local fighter Leonard Blanchard, who had a reported six wins, four defeats and five draws. Judd also had also scheduled a match for Shorty the following day against hard-punching Booker T. Washington on the Williams vs Marshall undercard. In the following weeks Judd hoped to arrange additional bouts for Shorty at small clubs in Sacramento and San Francisco as build-ups for a main event at San Francisco's Civic Auditorium. It was an ambitious program for any fighter coming back after a long lay-off, let alone a man in shorty's questionable physical and mental condition. The only obstacle standing in the way of Judd's plan was the not so small matter of a boxing license.

Either the members of the California boxing commission figured Shorty's 'Durocher Ear' condition rendered him ineligible for a license, or they discovered the real reason for his medical discharge from the Navy. Either way, they prevented what could only have ended in disaster since no license was issued, and no comeback was made. As a result,Shorty Hogue stepped away from the spotlight and quickly vanished from the public eye.

The non-event that was Shorty Hogue's comeback may have ignited something sinister in his psyche and, while surviving family members cannot (or will not) point at one particular incident, it seems that his level of control deteriorated. On Wednesday June 14, 1944, Shorty, Big Boy and a companion by the name of Louis Gazigli were arrested by the Washoe County Sheriff's office for their part in a brawl in a nightclub on the outskirts of Reno. Justice of the Peace Harry Dunseath set their bail at $200 apiece, which was paid, and they were released. Even though he was back in San Diego and away from the nefarious trappings of Reno, Big Boy couldn't stay out of trouble:

> "Charged with vagrancy, Willard (Big Boy) Hogue, 23, former professional boxer, entered a plea of not guilty when arraigned before Judge John J. Brennan yesterday. His trial was set for Municipal court Aug 23. Hogue was arrested early yesterday in a card room in the 110 block of Third Ave."

> —*San Diego Union*, August 13, 1944

While things looked bad for Big Boy, they grew increasingly bleak for Shorty as he was admitted to psychiatric facilities on a number of occasions during the following months. Looking back at the evidence of Shorty's condition - chronic traumatic encephalopathy - it is now apparent that his mental health issues were a symptom of the same.

In a paper entitled "The Need to Explore the Prevalence and Treatment of Acquired Brain Injury Among Persons With Serious and

Persistent Mental Illness," Kathleen Tourney, PhD, Psychology Department of William Paterson University, New Jersey, wrote the following:

> "Although individuals with acquired brain injuries may have different symptoms according to the location of their injuries, many brain injuries involve disturbances in the individual's ability to plan, organize, initiate, control impulses, attend, concentrate, problem solve and recall information (*Davis 2002*).
>
> These symptoms often overlap with symptoms of serious and persistent mental illnesses such as bipolar disorder, schizophrenia, and major depression (*McGuire, Burright, Williams & Donovick, 1998*)."

Shorty's behavior, coupled with what were then becoming frequent escapes from medical facilities, undoubtedly put strain on everyone. Lori (Dye) Grove, recounting a story told by her dad (Bob Dye) said that Shorty was escaping on a regular basis because he hated the hospital:

> "One time the cops in El Centro arrested him and put him in jail without a peep. Once he was in the cell, they told him that they were going to take him back to the hospital. He told them that if they tried, he would *'whip both of them without even trying.'*
>
> They obviously knew who he was, because they called my dad, who was also a cop at the time. My dad bought him ice cream (which was always his favorite food. . . . Shorty was so sweet). After a couple of ice creams, Shorty agreed to go back with them. One of the cops pulled out his handcuffs, and Shorty told him that if he wanted him to go with him, he had better put them away; he did."

—Lori (Dye) Grove

Finally, things got so serious that a drastic medical intervention was considered. In a paper entitled "Therapeutic Effectiveness and Social Context: The Case of Lobotomy in a California State Hospital, 1947-1954," Dr. Joel Braslow (University of California, Los Angeles) found that doctors in many medical and psychiatric institutions in California (particularly in the one he studied in Stockton) used the practice of lobotomy as a way of conserving an institution's precious staff resources. Patients who underwent the procedure were more often docile and compliant, and therefore much easier to deal with in terms of labor and time expended.

The procedure itself, pioneered by neurologists Egas Moniz and Walter Freeman, was brutal. Moniz speculated that, "fixed neuronal connections in the frontal lobes led to psychiatric disease and that disruption of these connections could lead to cure."

The "disruption" was achieved in a number of ways — one was to introduce multiple injections of alcohol into the frontal lobes in order to separate the frontal white matter. Another was to physically cut through the white matter with what was essentially an icepick.

Both versions required that the frontal lobes be accessed via the orbital cavity, literally piercing through the fragile bone with a hammer and icepick-type tool in order to carry out the lobotomy. Patients always woke up with a couple of stunning black eyes. The post-operative look would likely not have bothered Shorty to any great extent — typical post-combat fare for his most recent fights. The real effects would have been beneath the surface:

> "That operation on Shorty was about 1944. The family wondered why the operation was done.
>
> We were told it was to calm him down and not hurt anyone, but as far as we knew he never hurt anyone outside of the ring.

Big Boy is the one who needed the operation."

—Bob Dye

Even though Shorty stepped out of the spotlight, the same could not be said of his manager, Cliff Judd. Known around Reno clubs and gambling establishments as *'The Galloper,'* Judd had a shady reputation. He had, or claimed an interest in, a number of bars and was not above bending the rules slightly in order to keep the cash rolling in. While co-managing the 'Depot Bar' on Commercial Row - considered the 'Skid Row' of Reno - he operated a number of unlicensed poker games in one or more rooms of the building. In July 1944, the unlicensed poker games were the least of his problems as on the 17th he was arrested for disturbing the peace at the Silver Dollar Club. Apparently, Judd went quietly until he arrived at the station where he was informed the police officers were going to take a mug-shot. Then all hell broke loose, and it took four officers to get him in front of the camera; he was released on $500 bail.

In February 1945, Judd and his business partner Blaine Dupuis were the subject of charges brought by wholesale liquor suppliers Levy & Zetner. The firm claimed that Judd and Dupuis had been provided with $11,512.24 worth of liquor in June and July, 1944; liquor they had failed to pay for. The defendants claimed that they were willing to pay $3,538.15 for 20 cases of scotch and 117 cases of bourbon, but were not prepared to pay for the 50 cases of brandy and 87 cases of tequila that were forced upon them in a 'combination sale'. That is, in order to get the scotch and bourbon (always in high demand), they would have to buy the other liquor also. Combination sales were in breach of the OPA Price Control Act. These run-ins with the local authorities may have been another reason why Shorty's comeback stalled. Although the absence of a boxing licence in California would not necessarily disbar him from obtaining one in another state.

The court ordered that Judd and Dupuis return 60 cases of Estrella Polar, 39 cases of white tequila and 50 cases of St. Jaques brandy, and to pay $5,164.19 to the wholesalers, with court costs to be borne by both sides.

In April 1945, Judd was fined a total of $100 for not having a license to run 'craps' and '21' games at his establishment. Around the same time, the Federal Grand Jury returned two indictments against Judd for 'sale above ceiling prices' for 18 cases of whiskey for disposal in Salt Lake City. He was also fined for operating as a wholesaler without a liquor license.

Linked to the same offences were charges by the US Attorney in San Francisco for intimidating a government witness - Lester Haliman (a San Francisco bartender) - whom Judd was alleged to have beaten. Haliman and one William Bedly Jnr. were arrested at Elko on March 19 while en-route to Salt Lake City to dispose of the whiskey. Judd was found guilty and sentenced to six months in a San Francisco jail. Along with his liberty went his gaming license.

In February 1949, Judd and co-conspirator Warren Brewer appeared in what was, at the time, the longest trial in the history of the Las Vegas City Court. Both were charged with drilling a hole in the side of a slot machine and inserting plugs to make the machine pay off. They were spotted by bartender Guy Lutrell who raised the alarm. According to the March 12 edition of the *Billboard* (page121), Judd was fined $500 with the alternative of spending 250 days in jail. The attorney for Warren Brewer appeared satisfied with his client's $200 fine or 100 days in prison - stating that there would be no appeal.

Judd was in trouble again in May 1952 when he and two associates, Roy Nelson and Newt Baker, were arrested following the criminal destruction of a gaming table at the Frisco Club in Reno. Nelson, aided by Judd and Baker, poured acid onto the table while attempting to conceal their actions behind a newspaper. By the mid

1950s, Judd had seen enough of Reno, or else Reno had seen enough of Judd. Either way, he sold his latest venture - The Bar of Music - to former heavyweight title challenger Buddy Baer and relocated to the not so bright lights of Fairbanks, Nebraska where he continued his nefarious activities.

By 1955, Judd was operating the Dreamland Bar with partner Bugs Reeves. A year later, he was posting $30,000 in bail for Chicago mobsters after being arrested following a phoney construction paycheque scam which apparently cost local merchants in excess of $21,000. In 1957, Judd was buying property on 2nd Ave. in Fairbanks for the purpose of building a hotel. Later the same year, he got into a beef with one Jimmy Ing - a local hoodlum of some repute. Ing, who was allegedly involved in the aforementioned construction paycheque scam, was also operating in the area as a 'liquor sales-man' - as was Cliff Judd's old side-kick, Warren Brewer. According to the *Fairbanks Daily News-Miner* (May 10, 1957), Ing was attacked at the Fireside Club by Judd and Warren Brewer - the attack coming after Ing had struck a waitress at the nearby Polaris Lounge. Following the brawl, a .32 pistol was found on the floor. Judd claimed he had seen the gun in Ing's possession earlier in the day - which Ing denied.

It may have been smarter for Judd and Brewer to stay well clear of Jimmy Ing since he had a record and a reputation that made the Reno boys' exploits pale into insignificance. Originally from Peoria, Ill, Ing - who also went by the name of 'Robert Blue' - was mixed up with a serious group of people from Illinois. By the time he was 20, he was serving time in the state penitentiary in Pontiac and upon his release, had enlisted in the Army Air Services. By the end of November, 1945, Ing was a married man and may have been intent on remaining on the straight and narrow. But 10 years later he was orchestrating a fraudulent construction paycheque scam in Alaska on behalf of his Illinois associates. There is one story about Ing which tells how he took a baseball bat to a local hoodlum and clubbed him to within an inch of his life. He then put the guy into an oil drum, covered him with oil, and set him alight.

Ing was later convicted of the construction paycheque scam, though he managed to get his initial 15-year sentence overturned on appeal. He was not so lucky in escaping the charges of feloniously having a pistol, 20 counts of forgery, not having a liquor license, failure to maintain liquor sales records and not paying taxes. He appeared to accept the punishment as an occupational hazard and carried on as usual. Ing obviously upset many people and was dead before he reached 50; dying in a hail of bullets following a robbery and a police sting in Reno.

Cliff Judd remained in Fairbanks, Alaska for many years and always appeared to exist on the fringes of the law:

> "Judd was a card shark. My wife and I was in and out of Alaska for 10 years. I knew Cliff Judd. He was a friend of Nip Hogue. When a guy from Alaska told him who I was and told him I was from a fighting family, the Hogue twins, Judd asked him was I as crazy as the Hogues.
>
> Then Judd came over, and we talked a long time. I found out later that Judd was feared by most people he knew. I knew nothing for a fact, but he was in jail for a lot of things. Nip Hogue was a bad person too, they made a good pair.
>
> He [Judd] was sick when I was there in 1980. He was working for a fellow named Sam Jeffcoat and Jeffcoat was afraid of him. I spoke with Judd a few times, but the things I heard I did not want to know him."

—Bob Dye

Shorty Hogue alongside Cliff Judd.
The photo is signed and dated May 18, 1944 (Author's collection)

The Hogue brothers in happier times.
(Photo courtesy of Bob and Lori Dye).

CHAPTER TEN

B ig Boy seemed content to hang around with his buddies in Reno. Street brawls aside, neither of the twins caused so much as a ripple in the local press until June 13, 1951. Big Boy was arrested, along with his friend Harold Thomas, following a scuffle with authorities in an establishment called 'The West Indies' on South Virginia Road, Reno. Either Big Boy or Thomas had been seen palming a card during a game and, when challenged, they tried to fight their way out of an arrest.

Both men appeared in the local justice court where they originally pled not guilty to the charge of resisting arrest and were released on $400 bail pending a hearing. At the follow-up hearing, evidence was presented of organized card-cheating, showing how Big Boy and Thomas had in their possession equipment for fixing card decks. Both changed their plea and were sentenced to six months in jail if they were found in Reno after 4:00 pm on Thursday, June 29.

It appears that the symptoms of 'punch-drunk syndrome' were affecting Big Boy as much as Shorty; the difference was that Shorty had received an official diagnosis:

"Big Boy was very mean. He once hit a guy in a bar with a roll of quarters in his fist just to see if the roll would bust open. It did.

He was also in a bar in Las Vegas, Nevada. Big Boy walked up to a guy sitting on a stool and knocked him off the stool for no reason. Well, obviously a fight ensued and the guy got on top of Big Boy and started hitting him."

—Bob Dye

Willard's violent outbursts were not confined to barrooms or the street. Bob Dye said that " . . . sad, but true, Big Boy slapped his wife around and burnt her a couple of times with cigarettes."

According to most research papers addressing the study of chronic traumatic encephalopathy (CTE) in boxers, there are a number of common symptoms that tend to manifest themselves at various stages of the condition. Dementia, declining mental ability, lack of coordination, unsteady gait and speech problems are amongst the earlier signs.

The term 'punch drunk,' when referring to boxers and ex-boxers, was first coined by fight fans, promoters and fighters themselves many years before it was accepted by the medical fraternity. Many involved in the sport had recognized a peculiar condition occurring among prize fighters, whom in ring parlance, they would speak of as 'punch drunk,' 'cuckoo,' 'goofy' or 'slug nutty.'

In 1928, the pathologist Harrison Martland published a paper entitled "Punch Drunk":

"Many cases remain mild in nature and do not progress beyond this point. In others, a very distinct dragging of the leg may develop, and with this there is general slowing down in muscular movements, a peculiar mental attitude characterized by hesitancy in speech, tremors of the hands and nodding movements of the head, necessitating withdrawal from the ring.

Later on, in severe cases, there may develop a peculiar tilting of the head, a dragging of one or both legs, a staggering, propulsive gait with the facial characteristics of the parkinsonian syndrome, or a backward swaying of the body, tremors, vertigo and deafness. Finally, marked mental deterioration may set in necessitating commitment to an asylum.

Punch drunk most often affects fighters of the slugging type, who are usually poor boxers and who take considerable punishment, seeking only to land a knockout blow. It is also common in second rate fighters used for training purposes, who may be knocked down several times a day. Frequently it takes a fighter from one or two hours to recover from a severe blow to the head or jaw. In some cases consciousness may be lost for a considerable period of time.

The syndrome includes, as described, slurred speech, atactic disturbances and an impairment of psychic functions, all symptoms, which simulate an alcoholic intoxication."

Between 1935 and 1967 the eminent British neurologist, McDonald Critchley wrote of a number of conditions impacting boxers, in particular those affecting neurological and nervous disfunction. He indicated that punch drunkenness is found more often in profes-sionals than in amateurs, in the second- or third-rate performer rather than in the scientific exponent with a county or provincial title. As fighters, they are rarely quick on their feet, but are better known as able to 'take it.' He also noted that there is a direct ratio between the degree of facial scarring (cauliflower ears, broken nose, thickened eyebrow ridges) and the intensity of the punch-drunk symptoms. He concluded that from a potential brain damage perspective, being *'knocked out on their feet'* is more significant than being floored.

Additional documented symptoms of pugilistica dementia have included difficulty with impulse control, disinhibition, irritability, inappropriateness, excessive sexual demands, and explosive outbursts of anger and aggression. There may also be irrational jealousy and a suspicion of spousal infidelity, and increased sensitivity to the effects of alcohol. Just about every study into the condition indicates that difficulty with memory — especially with regard to events of little personal significance — is also a problem.

Barry D. Jordan (former Medical Director of the New York State Athletic Commission) collated a massive amount of previous medical research to compliment his own for his opus 'Medical Aspects of Boxing' (CRC Press: 1993). Citing research contained in the 1928 "Punch Drunk" paper by Harrison Martland, Jordan highlights evidence that a number of prominent fighters of the day had suffered severe mental and physical repercussions as a result of their profession. The shocking thing about Martland's research is the vast number of case studies showing former fighters who were listed as either "punch-drunk," "dragging one leg," "talking slowly," "in bad shape," or "in asylum."

In May 1952, Big Boy had an urge to enter the ring again. It had been over eight years since his last fight, and the reasoning behind his decision is unknown. It is possible that it was around this time that he got in some extra-curricular fisticuffs with his twin brother:

"Shorty would run away from the hospital every so often. This time Big Boy was home in El Centro and, being a big ass, like Big Boy was, he started a fight with Shorty. Shorty would not fight, mostly because of the operation he had at the hospital, and Big Boy beat Shorty very bad. I was not there, but was told about it. Throughout their lives, Shorty always got the best of Big Boy, so this was a payback."

—Bob Dye

Shorty received a cut eye and a badly cut lip and, according to Bob Dye, should really have gone to the hospital for treatment, but didn't. Simon was furious with Big Boy for taking advantage of their brother in such a fashion.

Whether or not Big Boy's decision to enter the ring again was based on ambition, one final chance to lay to rest some ghosts, or the irrational feeling that he deserved to be punished in some way, it could not have been considered sound thinking. The real reason may have been that his undiagnosed condition was impairing his judgement, thus causing the violent outbursts. Whatever way you look at the situation, the choices made were poor. So for his final hurrah, Big Boy Hogue headed to Phoenix, Arizona for one last roll of the dice:

"Jose Rocha, 157, Monterey, Mex., cut the left eye of big Boy Hogue, 157, Sand Diego, Calif., and the bout was stopped between the fourth and fifth rounds. The come-backing Hogue had waged a game battle until then."

—*Arizona Republic*, May 10, 1952

Perhaps encouraged by the *Republic*'s report, Big Boy decided to give it another go. On May 28th, the same publication reported that the two were due to fight again, and on May 30th a promotional piece in the *Republic stated* "a come-backing Big Boy Hogue is matched with Jose Rocha, who scored a TKO over him here three weeks ago." On June 1, a report in the same paper carried the result

- *Hank (Kid) Davis, 158, Phoenix won TKO 4 over Big Boy Hogue, 156, San Diego.* A second TKO loss in three weeks left Big Boy with few options regarding his future:

> "One veteran boxing observer, after watching Friday night's bouts, figures Big Boy Hogue and Bert (Cucamunga) Mendoza ought to drop their comeback plans immediately and hang up the ring togs. Hogue suffered his second straight TKO in three weeks when scar tissue over his eyes was opened up in a cut requiring four stitches.
>
> They just can't get in shape anymore."

> —*Arizona Republic*, June 1, 1952

Bob Dye was with Big Boy for the last fight in Phoenix. After the loss Dye took him to a local doctor to get patched up. It turned out to be an eye-opener for Big Boy's nephew:

> "Dad said that both of the twins used heroin. Dad drove Big Boy from one of his last fights, and his eye was cut open pretty badly. They stopped at a doctor's office and the doctor told Big Boy he was going to give him a pain shot. Big Boy laid down on the gurney and pushed his body way back so that his head dropped off of the edge. The doctor knew instantly that he was a drug user and commented on it."

> —Lori (Dye) Grove

The fights in Arizona were definitely the end of the line for Big Boy, just as the fights in San Diego more than nine years earlier had been the end of a relatively brief, but spectacular ride for Shorty. At 31 years old, both were still young men, but life had taken its toll on them. Shorty was living in a variety of care facilities, and Big Boy, who spent several years in and out of Atascadero Mental Hospital, appeared to have no discernible skills outside of the ring other than cheating at cards. He spent some time gainfully employed in the contracting business and as a longshoreman in San Diego, but regular work was hard to come by.

In August, 1958, Big Boy's daughter Sherry gave birth to her first child, a first granddaughter for Big Boy and Frances. Jimmie Hogue and his wife presented Big Boy with his first grandson in December 1958 and another granddaughter in November 1960. Sherry then produced another son in April, 1961. So many new lives and, one would hope, such joy for the family as a whole.

In October 1961, just over nine years after his last fight, Big Boy's world was turned upside-down. On Sunday the 22nd, Jimmie Hogue and his friend and former school buddy, Lester Ray Hudson, met up for some fun. Lester, a private based at Fort Lewis in Washington, was on leave from the Army, having enlisted practically straight out of El Cajon Valley High School.

Jimmie rode his motorcycle from his home on Los Coches Road, Lakeside to Lester's parents house just over six miles away on South Avocado Ave. in El Cajon. They then went out for a spin along US Highway 80 on the section known as Kumeyaay Highway. As the pair approached Flinn Springs Road, the bike and the boys collided with a car, and both boys were killed instantly. Jimmie Hogue was only 23 years old and left behind a wife and two infant children. Lester, still single, and only a year older, left behind distraught parents and siblings. The driver of the car survived.

Barely six months later, on April 18, 1962, Big Boy's wife died of breast cancer. Frances Hogue was only 43 years old. Mother and son were buried next to each other at Alpine Cemetery, around 30 miles east of San Diego, and there is little doubt that a large part of Willard 'Big Boy' Hogue was buried along with them.

And so, even as Shorty continued to languish in Sawtelle Veterans' Hospital in Los Angeles, his twin was battling new demons of his own. After the death of his wife and son, Big Boy was institutionalized on a number of occasions, and when he was not in hospital it seems he was left to drift. Following his latest period of 'observation,' he was allowed to live in a cabin at the back of his sister Jewell's home in Porterville:

> "Big Boy was living with my Grandmother because he had called her and asked her to take him out of Atascadero. She told him that if got into any trouble at all, she would take him back. He was suffering from severe depression and felt very alone."

> —Lori (Dye) Grove

On Tuesday June 17, 1964, Jewell gave Big Boy some money to go get a haircut in town. He was on his way back home to 1028 Sycamore Street at around 9.30 p.m. when he was arrested by police for being drunk in public. Bob Dye remembers that his mother Jewell went to the police station to explain that Big Boy couldn't have been drunk as he had no money. She also told them that because he walked on his heels a little, he gave the impression of being drunk. The police didn't or wouldn't listen and they decided to hold Big Boy until he had 'sobered up,' but he never did. Just before midnight, an officer went to check in on the prisoner. He found Big Boy hanging in his cell. He had used his own belt to end his life. He was only 43.

In a normal world, the next couple of weeks would have seen Big Boy's family celebrate the birthdays of his son Jimmie and his wife, but neither of them were here for him now. The joy of becoming a grandfather again (there were now six) could not dull the pain he must have been feeling - even if the latest arrivals were twin boys.

Nelson Fisher, writing about Big Boy's suicide for the *San Diego Tribune*, cited the twins as the reason behind the San Diego Coliseum enjoying its "vintage years" in attendances during the late 1930s and early '40s. And, in one paragraph, he summed up their lives and careers almost perfectly:

> "If their boxing careers were crowned by success and popularity, their lives after they put away the gloves were as contrastingly unfortunate, eventually tragic."

Willard 'Big Boy' Hogue was laid to rest on June 21, 1964, at Alpine Cemetery near El Cajon. His grave, marked by a black stone bearing his ring name and an outline of a pair of boxing gloves, is less than 15 feet from the place where his wife and son lay.

Boxing had taken a great deal from Big Boy Hogue - his youth, his health and his sense of place in the world - leaving him unable to cope with even the most ordinary aspects of life once the cheers had died down and the ring lights had been extinguished. Of course, he was not the first, nor would he be the last, to have paid a high price for fleeting moments of glory.

In his documentary film, *64 Day Hero* (1985) Gordon Williams investigates the life and death of Randolph (Randy) Turpin, the former middleweight champion from Great Britain. Tracking Turpin's 24 years of ring activity — beginning with his first ring appearances in a novelty act as a young boy, and then covering the rest of a career which included 70 amateur matches, 73 professional fights, countless exhibitions and boxing booth fights, and thousands of rounds of sparring — Williams explores whether Turpin's two months as champion was worth the pain he endured during his career, especially when his unfortunate post-boxing years and tragic death are taken into account.

The family novelty act to which Williams referred was a boxing routine featuring eight year-old Randy and his slightly older brother Jackie. The act, called 'Alexander and Moses' was designed by George Middleton, then manager of Dick Turpin, the much-older brother of the two boys. Middleton would outfit Jackie and Randolph in small boxing gloves and customized dressing gowns and shorts for the tiny boxers to play out their routine.

They would oppose each other as 'light entertainment' at tournaments that Dick Turpin was boxing on. Because neither Jackie nor Randy wanted to be humiliated in front of their big brother - or the paying public - they would attack each other in the most ferocious manner. Their battles were so entertaining, and they were showered with so many coins, that often their total purse for the night amounted to more than their brother Dick, who was fighting for a living.

Recent research into concussion and brain damage in sports indicates that there may be a genetic predisposition to pugilistic dementia, and a comparison of the careers and lives of the Hogues and Turpins lends some weight to this argument.

The boyhood experiences of the younger Turpin brothers and the Hogue twins were similar, although one of the Turpins did manage to scale the heights of his profession. Randy won the world middleweight championship from Sugar Ray Robinson in July 1951, only to lose the crown back to Robinson just 64 days later. Unable to capitalise on subsequent opportunities, Turpin also saw his fighting skills begin to erode at a relatively young age, with his mental health soon to follow. Plagued by financial problems and paranoia, he took his own life in May, 1966. However, in Turpin's case, the mental health and paranoia might have been more stress than punch-drunk related.

Maybe it was too many hard fights, maybe it was a case of too much, too soon, but Randy Turpin and Big Boy Hogue had been slinging leather since they were small boys, and the damage done to a young, developing brain must be considered as a possible factor in the demise of both men. The flip side in Turpin's case is that he was also under considerable pressure from the tax man and (according to some sources) from associates of British boxing impresario Jack Solomons, for whom he had allegedly smuggled huge amounts of cash into Britain following his New York title defense against Robinson. So too, Turpin had seemed normal enough to family members prior to the tragic events of May 1966, having displayed no obvious signs of pugilistic dementia. The other half of the 'Alexander and Moses' act, Jackie Turpin, showed no apparent ill-effects from his 125 fight boxing career and lived to be 84. Older brother Dick Turpin also survived with his senses intact, reaching age 69 despite having 107 pro fights.

Bob Dye remembers that he went to visit Shorty at a sanatorium in Saugus in order to break the news of Big Boy's passing, but he already knew:

"In later years, Shorty started quoting the Bible to people. When I visited him at VA I found him at a table I went over and sat by him, and he said to me a couple of things from the bible. I said, 'That's good Shorty.' He looked at me and said, 'Bob, how about buying me some ice-cream.' So, I did. He said, 'Big Boy killed himself.' I said, 'yes he did, how did you know?' He said, 'Everyone in the hospital knows it.' So I said, 'Jimmy died on a motorcycle with another kid and Frances died of breast cancer, and he did not want to take it any more.'"

—Bob Dye

"I was with my Dad in San Diego when he told Shorty that Big Boy committed suicide. True, I was very young, but I have an unbelievable memory. It was a hospital, but not the normal hospital. I know it was a VA now, but let me tell you what I heard and saw. There was a large courtyard in the middle of it. All of the way around the courtyard were rooms with large windows with screen openings. The rooms were four stories high all of the way around. When you walked into the courtyard, men were yelling all kinds of crazy things.

Shorty was already in the courtyard. He recognized my dad immediately. Within the first minute or so, Shorty asked my dad if Big Boy killed himself. Dad told him yes and that Big Boy was probably just tired since Francis and Jimmy had passed away.

Dad wrote (email) to me that Shorty didn't really care, he just wanted ice cream; that's not what happened. Shorty became really quiet, and you could tell he was reflecting as he was looking down at the ground. He slowly looked up and asked my dad for some ice cream. My dad went and got him some. While my dad was gone, Shorty insisted on asking us if we knew all of the capitals of all of the states. When my dad returned, Shorty's personality started to change.

Looking back on it now, with all of my experience with the mentally ill, I have to say, I've never seen anything like it. He started talking about how he was married five times, and what he would do if he had all five of them at the same time; it got so graphic that we left.

We never went back."

—Lori (Dye) Grove

Willis 'Shorty' Hogue remained in the care of the Veterans' Association for the rest of his life. First at Sawtelle, then later at a retirement facility in Saugus, north of Los Angeles in what is now Santa

Clarita. The rage and aggression that had fueled his incredible fighting career had long since been dissipated by a lobotomy that he most likely never needed.

What little remained of Shorty Hogue finally gave up the fight on November 29, 1971; he died in his sleep in a room he shared with another man at the Sleepy Valley Rest Home on Reservoir Street. Percy Brady, the owner of the establishment, told the Santa Clarita *Signal* that Shorty suffered a heart attack late on Monday. Firemen were unable to revive him, and he was later pronounced dead at the Inter-Valley Hospital. Brady also said that Shorty was almost penniless, adding "All of his medals got away from him somewhere."

Willis 'Shorty' Hogue was buried close to his parents in Evergreen Cemetery, El Centro, California. Bishop Robert Lamoreaux of the El Centro Church of Latter-day Saints presided over the graveside service.

Old Highway 80, Jacumba Hot Springs, California
(Photograph from article in the San Diego Reader - 2016)

The Jacumba Hotel was situated near the telegraph poles on the left and the white building on the right was previously the site of the D & B Cafe.

AFTERWORD

The spa town of Jacumba sits in a valley amongst the Jacumba Mountains 2,800 feet above sea-level. It is situated on the border with Mexico, less than half a mile from the small settlement of La Rumerosa. San Diego is around 75 miles to the west, and El Centro is 50 miles to the east.

At the end of 2018, the once booming town is now almost desolate. Depending on whose estimate you believe, some 250 to 500 people – mostly painters, writers, musicians, and photographers – call the place home. With no attractions to speak of, and little to recommend it outside of refuelling, a comfort break or a photo opportunity at the Chinese Castle, or the Mountain View Tower, it is the ideal place to hide from the world. Which is just what some inhabitants do.

With a massive break in the U. S.–Mexican border fence, it was also — until quite recently — the ideal illegal pathway onto US soil from the South. Locals speak of whispered voices and hushed footsteps outside their properties in the small hours - refugees from

Rumerosa tip-toeing their way into the land of the free. With a wall now being constructed, things will no doubt change.

The Jacumba Hotel is gone, abandoned by the owners and then destroyed in a fire in 1983. Only the fireplace and a nub of the chimney remain — a ghostly sentinel standing guard amid the brush and scrub of a desert landscape.

The Barbara Worth Cafe is now the Mountain Sage Market, and the D & B Cafe — most recently a tattoo parlor — stands abandoned. The former pharmacy and drug store on the corner of Jacumba Street is the only building on the block that has recently shown signs of life. Further west, along old Highway 80, one of the spas has again seen a small increase in tourist activity.

Jacumba, like everything else, is not what it used to be, even the name has changed.— now 'Jacumba Hot Springs', perhaps in the vain hope of sounding more attractive. The thriving spa town that brought in Clark Gable and co. will never again see such days. No longer an oasis in the desert for Hollywood stars and their ilk, and no longer the centre of the universe for two young boys who beat each other raw for pennies on a corralled piece of land, or who raced up Mount Jacumba - neither one wanting to be last to the top.

The twins' favourite stomping ground, the San Diego Coliseum, has also faded into memory. The last professional fight card there was December 19, 1979. Besides the 100-plus times the twins fought there, the venue had also hosted world champions Chalky Wright, Manuel Ortiz (of nearby El Centro), Ken Norton and the Ol' Mongoose himself, Archie Moore. The final two fighters to step through the ropes were David Madrid and 'Spud' Murphy - 'Ham and Eggers' with less than 25 fights between them.

When the doors closed for the final time, Danny Milsap - the last man to promote boxing at the Coliseum - told reporter Wayne

Lockwood, "When the twins were fighting, if you didn't get to the Coliseum by 6 p.m., you weren't going to get in." The venue became a furniture store for many years. It has recently been incorporated into the area's 'urban regeneration' program.

"Man, they looked like movie actors," Milsap also said of the twins. He was not wrong. Shorty was once mistaken by a crowd in a Porterville pool hall for actor John Garfield. Shorty told Bob Dye, whose father operated the establishment, that he thought he was better looking than Garfield - Bob agreed.

"They had charisma. They were just beautiful kids," added Milsap. Reporter Burdette Kinne, who covered the twins' amateur careers said, "They would have made a mint, even in these days. But they weren't handled too well. Shorty fought way too often - they just used him up; it was a real waste."

Archie Moore also remembered Shorty and Big Boy with great affection. He told Jerry Magee of the *San Diego Union Tribune* (April 7, 1993), "They were good mixers, they would fight you off your feet. They came to fight, and that's why the people loved them so. They tolerated me."

In a personal letter to the twins' nephew, Richard Plummer, (July, 1993) Moore wrote:

"The twins were sure two of the greatest prospects in my time, they had everything needed to be world champions, well maybe one thing was missing — patience".

THOUGHTS AMONG THE RESIN

Yes, there's glamor to it, when you're up around the top;

Yes, there's something to it while the other fellows drop;

But some day when the tide has turned, some bitter battle when,

You snuggle in the resin while some bloke is counting ten,

Oh, it's something different then.

To lie there with a battered face where many time before

You'd seen your rival resting as his features spouted gore,

To see him standing over you all set if you should rise

To let you have some more of it between your blinking eyes,

As he reaches for your prize.

To see gray phantoms of the past drift back across the years,

To hear the haunting echo of a thousand roaring cheers,

To know you'll never hear again the plaudits and acclaim

That only rise for those who still are rulers of the game,

In the fickleness of fame.

To lie there in the resin and to know your time is done,

To know your final scrap is in, your final race is run;

To know the tide has turned at last, some bitter battle when

You snuggle in the bloody dust while some one's counting ten—

Oh, you pay for it then.

—Grantland Rice

(Reproduced from the Evening Public Ledger,—Philadelphia. July 14, 1919)

Willis Burton Hogue
"Shorty"

December 26, 1920 - Skiatook, Oklahoma
November 29, 1971 - Saugus, California

(Amateur Record)
San Diego Athletic Club
1939 National Diamond Belt Middleweight Champion

Bouts listed as: Date - Opponent - Club/location (if known) - Result

1936

Jun 2: Robert Adams KO4
Jun 9: Mayo Sario W4
Jun 30: Al Flores KO4
Johnnie Aguilar KO2
Jul 21: Cleo Shans (Bawley AC) W4
Jul 28: Joe Murio W4
Robert Adams W4

Luis Ruiz (Old Town) KO3

Billy Cardenis W4

Cleo Shans (Bawley AC) W4

Oct 29: Fred Koch (USS Dale) W4

Kid Buddy W4

Luis Ruiz (Old Town) KO1

Billy Potts (USS Tennessee) KO2

Tommy Gonzalez (CAC) W4

1937

Henry Martinez (Sherman) W4

Feb 8: Joe Garcia W4

Mar 1: Johnny Jarred (USS Fox) KO3

Mar 8: Cotton Whitaker (Texas) W4

Mar 22: Tommy Gonzalez (CAC) W4

Apr 13 McKinley Stokes KO3

Apr 20: Bill White (Bawley AC) W4

Apr 26: Battling Nick (CAC) KO2

Apr 29: Don Benzor (El Centro) W4

May 4: Jess Gonzalez KO3

May 20: Henry Martinez (Sherman) W4

May 24:Frankie Genaro (Elsinore) KO1

Joe Guerro KO2

Jun 14: Marcus Ray W4

Tony Devo KO4

Jun 22: Uley Harris LTKO3 *(cut eye)*

July: Uley Harris WDQ4

Eddie Maresette W4

Willie Fields W4

Jul 27: Luis Ruiz TKO3

Aug 10: Wilson Mackey W4

Aug 17: Chico Madrid KO3

Aug 24: Wilson Mackey W4

Lt Weight Championship Ca.
Sep 16: Joe Villegas (El Centro) W4
Sep: Miller Fonseca LD4

1938

Sep 2: Ivan Lewis KO2
Sep 9: Richard Earl KO1
O'Hara Chivez KO4
Sep 22: Kent Roberts W4
Oct: Ray Valarde W4
Oct 14: Alfred Moranda KO4
Oct: O'Shannon Chavez W4
Oct 27: Billy Mitchell W4
Jose Cabrero KO3
Nov 4: Bill O'Malley (Los Angeles) W4
Nov 16: Ray Valarde W4*
Nov 16: Frankie Jackson W4*

Shorty fought two opponents on one night when Big Boy could not compete due to a hip injury

Nov 18: Johnnie Flores KO1
Nov 30: William Gugler KO2*
Dec 1: Colbert Broussard (Bakersfield) KO2*
Johnnie Wilkes W4*
Dec 4: Jimmie Coleman W4*
Dec 4: Willie Collins KO3*
Dec 5: Sammy Nero W4*
LA Examiner Golden Gloves
Dec 20: Ken Wren KO 1**
**Tri-City Golden Gloves Final
Dec: Ray Paddock W (result unconfirmed)

1939

Jimmie Coleman W4
Jan 17: Jimmie Coleman W4
Jan 18: Jessie Alfaro (Ontario, CA) W4
James Toney (Detroit) W4$^+$
Jan 27: Vince Fratello (New York) W4$^+$
+*Finals of Hearst National Diamond Belt (Middleweight)*
Luis Ruiz (Old Town) KO2

* * *

Total: 66
Won Points: 38
Won KO: 26
Lost Points: 1
Lost KO: 1
WDQ: 1
LDQ: 0

Willard Joseph Hogue
"Big Boy"

December 26, 1920 - Skiatook, Oklahoma
June 17, 1964 - Porterville, California

(Amateur Record)
San Diego Athletic Club
1939 National Diamond Belt Welterweight Champion

Bouts listed as: Date - Opponent - Club/location (if known) - Result

1936

May 25: Pete Lugo TKO3
Jun 2: Harry Arrington W4
9-Jun: Joe Moriset W4
Jun 30: Julio Martinez TKO3
Rochos. Rojas KO2
Jul 21: Joe Gonzales W4
Jul 28: Dave Guererro TKO2

Joe Garcia L4

Tuffy Loudermilk W4

Sep 4: Joe Rivers TKO4

Joe Garcia W4

Oct 29: Hal Rickards L4

Johnny O'Malley W4

Fred Cook TKO3

Tuffy Loudermilk (Holtville) W4

1937

Feb 8: Fred Koch W4

Tommy Young L4

Mar 1: Steve Garcia (Tijuana) TKO3

Mar 8: Billy Potts (USS Tennessee W4

Mar 22: Cotton Whitaker (Texas) TKO4

Mar 27: Cotton Whitaker (Texas) KO3

Apr 14: Bill White W4

Apr 20: Jimmy Lyon TKO2

Apr 26: Tommy Gonzales (CAC) TKO3

Joe Villegas W4

Imperial Valley LW Title

May 4: Albert Medrano KO3

May 20: Fred Young W4

May 24: Johnny O' Malley W4

Jun 14: Henry Martinez W4

Jun 15: Johnny Castillo W4

Jun 22: Johnny Castillo W4

Wilson Mackey L4

Cleo McNeil L4

1938

Sep 2: Vic Villavincencia (Calexico) W4

Sep 9: Clem Waske (El Centro AC) TKO2

Frank Zorrita W4

Sep 22: Martin Vasquez W4

Gus Gonzales W4

Oct 11: Pete Martinez W4

Oct 14: Gabby Sales (Burbank) W4

Oct 27: Al Higgs (El Centro AC) KO3

Nov 4: Chick Lawes (Los Angele) TKO4

Nov 18: Luis Ruiz KO4

Nov 29: Jack Thompson (Lompoc) W4*

Nov 30: Bob Cramer W4*

Dec 1: Ray Harrison (Unattached) W/O*

Dec 4: Cecil Hudson W4*

Dec 5: Art Gonzales W4*

LA Examiner Golden Gloves

Dec: Alonzo Williams W4

Dec 19: Jack Lunny W4**

Dec 20: Dale Maloney Olympic Audit W4**

**Tri-City Golden Gloves Finals*

1939

Jan 17: *Alonzo Williams W4*

Jan 18 Jesse James Jackson (Ontario, CA) L4

Joe Cabrerra W4

Al Priest W4+

Jan 27: Harold Smith (Detroit) W4+

+Finals of Hearst National Diamond Belt (Welterweight)

Feb: Bud Cramer: (Ocean Park) CAC W4

* * *

Total: 57
Won Points: 34
Won KO: 16
Lost Points: 6
Lost KO: 0
W/O (won via walk over): 1

The amateur records of both Hogue twins have been taken from family records (most bouts undated) and have been supplemented by newspaper (scrapbook) reports - some of which did not contain dates - and online newspaper archive reports

YEAR	NAME	FIGHTS	WON (KO/TKO)	LOST (KO/TKO)	DQ (W/L)	ROUNDS FOUGHT	Win %	KO %
1936	SHORTY	15	9 (6)	0	0	52	100	40
1936	BIG BOY	15	7 (6)	2 (0)	0	54	87	46
1937	SHORTY	25	13 (9)	1 (1)	1 (W)	87	92	22
1937	BIG BOY	18	9 (6)	3 (0)	0	69	83	33
1938	SHORTY	20	10 (10)	0	0	71	100	50
1938	BIG BOY	17	13 (4)	0	0	65	100	23
1939	SHORTY	6	5 (1)	0	0	22	100	20
1939	BIG BOY	6	5 (0)	1 (0)	0	24	80	0
Ama Totals	SHORTY	66	38 (26)	1 (1)	0	232	97	41
Ama Totals	BIG BOY	56	33 (16)	6 (0)	0	212	89	33

Shorty and Big Boy Hogue - Amateur boxing records: 1936-1939

Willis Burton Hogue
"Shorty"

(Professional Record)
California State Middleweight Champion

Bouts listed as: Date - Opponent - location - Result

1939

Mar 3: Al Jimenez San Diego, CA W TKO 3

Mar 10: Hut Thompson San Diego, CA W TKO 1

Mar 14: Ray Vargas Los Angeles, CA W PTS 6

Mar 24: Miller Fonseca San Diego, CA W TKO 4

Mar 31 Milton Kell San Diego, CA W TKO 6

Apr 10: Tommy Garland Santa Monica L TKO 3

Apr 28: O'Dell Mason San Diego, CA W TKO 6

May 5: Karl Lester San Diego, CA W PTS 6

May 12: Karl Lester San Diego, CA W PTS 6

May 19: Hughie Myatt San Diego, CA W PTS 6

Jun 29: Carmen Georgino El Centro, CA W TKO 3

Jul 7: Jimmy Gleason San Diego, CA W PTS 6

Jul 14: Homer Slack San Diego, CA W TKO 4

Jul 28: Johnny Folio San Diego, CA W PTS 6

Aug 11: Jack Taylor San Diego, CA W KO 1

Aug 18: Jimmy Brott San Diego, CA W TKO 2

Aug 25: Carlos Garcia San Diego, CA W KO 4

Sep 8: Tommy Garland San Diego, CA L TKO 2

Sep 25: Tommy Garland Santa Monica, CA W PTS 6

Oct 3: Chuey Vargas Los Angeles, CA W PTS 6

Oct 6: Art Johnson San Diego, CA W PTS 6

Oct 13: Art Saxell San Diego, CA W PTS 6

Oct 20: Billy Mitchell San Diego, CA W PTS 6

Dec 29: Archie Moore San Diego, CA W PTS 6

1940

Jan 12: Bobby Pacho San Diego, CA W PTS 10

Jan 19: Charley Simpson San Diego, CA W PTS 10

Mar 15: Johnny 'Bandit' Romero San Diego, CA W PTS 6

Mar 25: Bobby Pacho Santa Monica, CA W PTS 8

Mar 29: Jimmy Casino San Diego, CA W PTS 6

Apr 12: Johnny 'Bandit' Romero San Diego, CA W PTS 8

Apr 26: Angelo Puglisi San Diego, CA W TKO 7

May 10: Petey Mike San Diego, CA W KO 2

May 17: Johnny Jackson San Diego, CA W PTS 6

May 31: Johnny Jackson San Diego, CA W PTS 6

Jun 7: Lige Drew San Diego, CA D 6

Jun 14: Otto Blackwell San Diego, CA W PTS 10

Jun 21: Lige Drew San Diego, CA W TKO 9

Jul 5: Rand Jackson San Diego, CA W TKO 6

Jul 12: Earl Stevenson San Diego, CA W TKO 2

Sep 27: Bert Velasquez San Diego, CA W KO 3

Oct 7: Billy Latka San Francisco, CA W PTS 10

1941

Jan 3: Charley Harris San Diego, CA W TKO 5

Jan 10: Mac MacAbee San Diego, CA W TKO 2

Jan 31: Archie Moore San Diego, CA W PTS 10

Feb 7: Lloyd Marshall Sacramento, CA W PTS 10

Feb 26: Al Globe San Bernardino, CA W KO 3

Mar 14: Eddie Booker San Diego, CA D 10

May 2: Eddie Booker San Diego, CA L PTS 10

Jun 9: Lloyd Marshall Sacramento, CA L PTS 10

Aug 1: Ray Acosta Hollywood, CA W TKO 5

Aug 8: Bobby Pacho San Diego, CA W PTS 10

Aug 22: Eddie Booker San Diego, CA W PTS 10

Sep 19: Vern Earling San Diego, CA W PTS 10

Oct 24: Johnny Barbara Chicago, IL W TKO 8

Nov 7: Andre Jessurun Chicago, IL W TKO 7

Dec 19: Young Gene Buffalo San Diego, CA W TKO 5

1942

Jan 9: Charley Burley Minneapolis, MN L TKO 10

Feb 27: Joe Sutka Chicago, IL W PTS 10

Apr 24: Jack Coggins San Diego, CA L TKO 9

May 29: Al Callahan San Diego, CA W KO 5

Jun 12: Bobby Birch San Diego, CA L TKO 7

Jul 24: Bobby Birch San Diego, CA L TKO 3

Aug 14: Eddie Booker San Diego, CA L TKO 8

Sep 11: Johnny 'Bandit' Romero San Diego, CA L TKO 6

Oct 30: Archie Moore San Diego, CA L TKO 2

* * *

Total: 65
Won Points: 28
Won KO/TKO: 24
Lost Points: 2
Lost KO/TKO: 9
Draws: 2

Willard Joseph Hogue
"Big Boy"

(Professional Record)

Bouts listed as: Date - Opponent - location - Result

1939

Mar 3: George Romero San Diego, CA W PTS 6

Mar 10: Bobby Espinoza San Diego, CA W PTS 6

Mar 14: Dave Chacon Los Angeles, CA W PTS 6

Mar 24: George Romero San Diego, CA W KO 1

Mar 31: Jackie Leonard San Diego, CA W KO 5

Apr 10: Red Green Santa Monica, CA W PTS 6

Apr 14: Kenny Reed San Diego, CA W PTS 6

May 5: Angus Smith San Diego, CA W KO 4

May 12: Henry Majcher San Diego, CA W PTS 6

May 15: Uli Harris El Centro, CA W PTS 6

May 19: Kid Lester San Diego, CA W PTS 6

Jun 2: Johnny Verdusco San Diego, CA W TKO 3

Jun 9: Jack Rainwater San Diego, CA W TKO 1

Jun 16: Jesse James Jackson San Diego, CA W PTS 6

Jun 22: Bobby Pacho El Centro, CA W PTS 10

Jul 21: Ray Vargas El Centro, CA W PTS 6

Jul 28: Aaron (Al) Smith San Diego, CA W PTS 6

Aug 4: Chuey Vargas San Diego, CA W PTS 6

Aug 11: Chuey Vargas San Diego, CA W PTS 6

Aug 18: Aaron (Al) Smith San Diego, CA W PTS 6

Aug 25: Jesse James Jackson San Diego, CA W PTS 6

Sep 15: Tommy Garland San Diego, CA W PTS 6

Sep 25: Babe Hernandez Santa Monica, CA W PTS 6

Oct 3: Everett Simington Los Angeles, CA W PTS 6

Oct 6: Johnny Freitas San Diego, CA D 6

Oct 27: Nick Massiello San Diego, CA W PTS 6

Nov 3: Billy Mitchell San Diego, CA W PTS 6

Nov 10: Jimmy Johnson San Diego, CA W TKO 3

Nov 17: Tabby Romero San Diego, CA W PTS 6

Dec 8: Herman Graves San Diego, CA W TKO 3

Dec 26: Turkey Thompson Los Angeles, CA L KO 3

1940

Jan 5: Baby Face Robinson San Diego, CA W PTS 6

Feb 16: Jimmy Casino San Diego, CA D 6

Feb 19: Toots Bernstein Santa Monica, CA W PTS 6

Mar 1: O'Dell Mason San Diego, CA W KO 4

Mar 8: Jimmy Casino San Diego, CA L TKO 4

Apr 5: Baby Face Robinson San Diego, CA W PTS 6

Apr 9: Johnny Jackson Los Angeles, CA L PTS 6

Apr 19: Johnny Jackson San Diego, CA D 10

Apr 26 Nick Massiello Hollywood, CA W TKO 5

May 10: Lige Drew San Diego, CA D 6

May 24: Jimmy Lakes Hollywood, CA W TKO 4

Jun 7: Aaron (Al) Smith Hollywood, CA L PTS 10

Jul 5: Chuey Vargas San Diego, CA W PTS 10

Jul 19: Georgie Crouch San Diego, CA D 10

Aug 19: Fred Apostoli San Francisco, CA L PTS 10

Oct 7: Larry Derrick San Francisco, CA W TKO 4

Oct 24: Freddie Dixon Phoenix, CA W PTS 10

Dec 20: Aaron Wade San Francisco, CA L TKO 8

1941

Jan 24: Jimmy Casino San Diego, CA L KO 2

Feb 7: Paulie Watkins Sacramento, CA D 6

Feb 26: Pancho Ramirez San Bernardino, CA W PTS 8

Mar 7: Jimmy Casino San Diego, CA W PTS 10

Mar 28: Jack Hill San Diego, CA W PTS 10

Apr 22: Allen Matthews Seattle, WA L TKO 7

Aug 8: Charley Harris San Diego, CA W TKO 4

Aug 15: Freddie Dixon San Diego, CA W KO 4

Sep 12: Bernie Cardenas San Diego, CA W KO 3

Oct 24: Mike Sopko Chicago, IL W TKO 5

Nov 7: George Mitchell Chicago, IL W TKO 8

Dec 19: Bobby Birch San Diego, CA L TKO 2

1942

Feb: 13 Charley Burley San Diego, CA L TKO 6

Apr 10: Billy Metcalf San Diego, CA W KO 3

Apr 17: Johnny 'Bandit' Romero San Diego, CA L TKO 9

Jul 10: Cecilio Lozada San Diego, CA W PTS 10

Jul 21: Jack Chase Los Angeles, CA L PTS 8

Sep 18: Eddie Booker San Diego, CA L TKO 4

Oct 2: Billy Beauhuld San Diego, CA L PTS 10

1943

Mar 19: Dick Ritchie San Diego, CA W TKO 8

Jul 22: Archie Moore San Diego, CA L TKO 5

Sep 17: Kid Lester San Diego, CA D 10

Sep 24: Billy Morris San Diego, CA L PTS 10

Nov 4: Battling Monroe San Diego, CA NC 2

Dec 10: Rusty Payne San Diego, CA L TKO 1

1944-1951
(Inactive)

1952

May 9: Jose Rocha Phoenix, AZ L TKO 4

May 31 Hank Davis Phoenix, AZ L TKO 3

* * *

Total: 75
Won Points: 31
Won KO/TKO: 18
Lost Points: 6
Lost KO/TKO: 13
Draws: 7

YEAR	NAME	FIGHTS	WON (KO)	LOST (KO)	DREW	NO CONTEST	DQ	ROUNDS FOUGHT	Avg WEIGHT	OPP Avg WEIGHT	OPP Win %	HOGUE Win %
1939	SHORTY	24	22 (11)	2 (2)	0	0	0	111	157	156	51	92
1939	BIG BOY	30	29 (7)	0	1	0	0	165	149	148	60	100
1940	SHORTY	17	16 (6)	0	1	0	0	115	156	158	74	94
1940	BIG BOY	17	8 (4)	5 (2)	4	0	0	119	157	153	75	47
1941	SHORTY	15	12 (7)	2 (0)	1	0	0	115	162	161	71	80
1941	BIG BOY	12	8 (5)	3(3)	1	0	0	69	159	158	75	66
1942	SHORTY	9	2 (2)	7 (7)	0	0	0	60	164	160	70	22
1942	BIG BOY	7	2 (1)	5 (3)	0	0	0	50	161	161	78	29
1943	SHORTY	N/A	N/A	N/A	N/A	N/A	0	N/A	N/A	N/A	N/A	N/A
1943	BIG BOY	6	1 (1)	3 (2)	1	1	0	36	160	160	67	17
1952	SHORTY	N/A	N/A	N/A	N/A	N/A	0	N/A	N/A	N/A	N/A	N/A
1952	BIG BOY	2	0	2 (2)	0	0	0	7	157	158	55	0
Pro Totals	SHORTY	65	52 (24)	11 (9)	2	0	0	401	159	159	67	80
Pro Totals	BIG BOY	74	48 (18)	18 (12)	7	1	0	446	154	154	68	65

Shorty and Big Boy Hogue - Pro boxing records: 1939-1952

	COMMON	SHORTY	BIG BOY
	OPPONENT	RESULTS	RESULTS
Bobby Birch		LTKO7-LTKO3	LTKO2
Eddie Booker		D10-LP10-W10-LTKO8	LTKO4
Charley Burley		LTKO10	LTKO6
Jimmy Casino		WP6	D6-LTKO6-LKO4-WP10
Lige Drew		D6-WTKO9	D6
Tommy Garland		LTKO3-LTKO2-WP6	WP6
Charley Harris		WTKO6	WTKO4
Johnny Jackson		WP6-WP6	LP6-D10
Billy Mitchell		WP6	WP6-WP6-WP10
Archie Moore		WP6-WP10-LTKO2	LTKO5
Bobby Pacho		WP10-WP8-WP10	WP10
Johnny 'Bandit' Romero		WP6-WP6-LTKO6	LTKO9
Chuey Vargas		WP6	WP6-WP6-WP10
TOTALS		Won-16 - Lost - 9 - Drew-2	Won-10 - Lost - 8 - Drew-3
OVERALL WIN %		59%	48%
Win % determined by number of fights (27 for Shorty - 21 for Big Boy)		31.17	20.23
Win % Determined by number of opponents (13)		64.74	32.69

Comparison of Twin's Results vs Common Opponents.

	SHORTY	BIG BOY
OPPONENT	RESULTS	RESULTS
Eddie Booker	D10-LP10-W10-LTKO8	LTKO4
Charley Burley	LTKO10	LTKO6
Jack Chase	N/A	LP8
Lloyd Marshall	WP10-LP10	N/A
Archie Moore	WP6-WP10-LTKO2	LTKO5
Aaron Wade	N/A	L-RET-8
TOTALS	Won-4 - Lost - 5 - Drew 1	Won-0 - Lost - 5
OVERALL WIN %	44%	0%

Twins' Results vs Murderers' Row

SCRAPBOOK CLIPPINGS

It's tough to ask you to look at this after a Saturday night. But these two lads head tomorrow's amateur fight card at the Coliseum and they're not only brothers but twins. They are the Hogue twins from Jacumba. On the left is Shorty. No, no. Pull yourself together, that's Big Boy. Or is that Big Boy on the right? Well.

The New Champ?

Bigboy Hogue, who meets Joe Villegas for the lightweight championship of Imperial and San Diego counties Thursday night, is shown as he gets in shape for the all important battle.

The twins prior to Shorty's third round kayo of Luis Ruiz (mid 1936) and Big Boy in April, 1937 prior to his meeting with Joe Villegas (bottom).

Replician Ringmasters

Pictured above are Jacumba's famous Hogue twins, Willard "Bigboy" Hogue at left, and Willis "Shorty" Hogue. The twins are slated to trade punches with San Diego's best in the Coliseum Monday night.

SHORTY AND BIG BOY HOGUE
TO FEATURE S. D. RING CARD

The twins around February, 1937 (above) and below with Jim Thorpe - also a twin and also part Native American - prior to the Pacific Coast finals December, 1938.

(Top) Big Boy on the way to defeating Art Gonzales during the *LA Examiner* Golden Gloves and (Bottom) Shorty has Ken Wren on the canvas in the first round of their Tri-City final (December, 1938)

TWIN HOWITZERS—The Mike and Ike of the Examiner Golden Gloves tournament are Willard and Willis Hogue of Jacumba. Both won their bouts in sensational style Monday night and will see action again tomorrow night. After the picture was taken, the photographer asked the twins to identify themselves. Willard said he was on right, but Willis said no, he was on right. The photog sneaked away while boys were still arguing, and there matter rests.
—Los Angeles Examiner photo

HOLLYWOOD BOUND?

FROM FIGHTERS TO FACE MAKERS is the likely step for the Hogue twins, Willis and Willard. The pair recently attracted national attention and offers from several studios after winning Examiner Golden Gloves championships. They fight again next Monday night at the Olympic in the Tri-City tournament. Study them closely and see if you can tell the welterweight, or 147-pounder, from the middleweight, 160 pounds. You're probably wrong. Willard (Shorty), the welter, is on the left. Willis (Big Boy), the middleweight, is on the right.
—Los Angeles Examiner photo

Both reports published during *LA Examiner* Golden Gloves (December, 1938). The bottom photo is immediately prior to the Tri-City finals (the report has the twins the wrong way around in the caption).

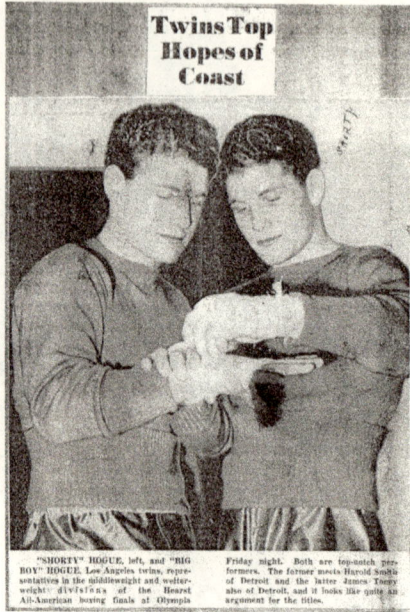

(Top) The twins wrapping their hands prior to the national semi-finals in Detroit (January, 1939) and (bottom) after winning their finals at the same event.

(Top) Post national finals with Detroit motor chief, Harry Bennett and (bottom) the twins prior to entering the tournament in November, 1938.

"BLOSSOMING OUT as professional fighters tonight at the Olympic Auditorium are the sensational Hogue twins, Willis and Willard. Their cousin hitch-hiked his way here from Oklahoma to furnish the music for their serenade of sock. Left to right are, Willis (Shorty), national middleweight amateur champ, Trainer George Barnett, Willard (Big Boy), national welterweight champ, and cousin Bill Hayes."

LA Examiner, March 14, 1939

THIS WAS THE AMATEUR FAREWELL FOR JACUMBA'S HOGUE TWINS

Willie "Shorty" Hogue, floors Louie Soto (left and right). Willard "Big Boy" crosses a right that caps the career of Bud Cramer. That's the picture story of the fighting Hogue twins' last amateur boxing bouts. Tonight they launch professional careers at the Coliseum Athletic club in a twin, six-round main event. They draw tough fans in their debuts. (Paul Modgan photos).

Hogue Twins in Pro Debuts Tonight

Is Big Boy Hogue, the welterweight of the Jacumba twins, ready to start taking pot shots at the

BIG BOY HOGUE
. . . is he ready yet?

crowned heads of the ring, or does he require more seasoning against the same class opponents he has been meeting for the last six or eight months?

OLYMPIC
Tues. Nite

Turkey
Thompson

vs.

Bigboy
Hogue

This figures
to be
one of the
best bouts
of 1939

THE HOGUE TWINS
BIGBOY AND SHORTY

These colorful lads, now under the management
of George Barnett of San Diego, are ready for
the big time. Bigboy boxes Turkey Thompson
at the Olympic Tuesday; Shorty faces Archie
Moore at San Diego Friday night

THE BLACK TIGER

Thompson is a club-fighter de luxe. Fans "go"
for his perpetual motion style. Manager Gayne
Norton likes Turkey to kayo Hogue.

TURKEY THOMPSON
Watch This Tiger in 1940

The *Knockout* - December 30, 1939 (back cover)
(Facing page) the twins from the *Knockout* (1941 and 1942)

SHORTY HOGUE

THE CALIF. MIDDLEWEIGHT CHAMPION

Shorty won the title by beating Eddie Booker.

Hogue dares Ceferino Garcia to fight him. Shorty is also after Seattle's Harry Matthews or any middleweight in the country.

The Hogue Twins are managed by Tom Jones, San Diego, Calif.

BIG BOY HOGUE

A club-fighting middleweight—will fight anything on two feet.

SPORTS

THE TRIBUNE SUN

HOW THEY COMPARE

MOORE		HOGUE
74 in.	reach	73 in.
15 in.	biceps	15 in.
13 in.	forearm	12½ in.
12½ in.	fist	12¾ in.
9 in.	ankle	9½ in.
15 in.	calf	16 in.
21 in.	thigh	22¾ in.
8 in.	wrist	8 in.
16 in.	neck	16¾ in.
35½ in.	chest (n)	40 in.
41 in.	chest (ex)	44½ in.
30¾ in.	waist	31 in.
5 ft. 11 in.	height	5 ft. 9½ in.
159 lbs.	weight	162 lbs.
23	age	26

"SHORTY" HOGUE

ARCHIE MOORE

As the comparative figures in the table above show, these two middleweights are astonishingly even in physical equipment. When they meet tonight in the Coliseum Athletic club's 10-round headliner, both will be gunning for the state championship, at which the winner has been promised a crack. Moore is a slight favorite because of greater experience and a more impressive record, being rated third in the list of middles. Hogue, however, has plenty of backing.—(Tribune staff photo.)

Shorty Hogue vs Archie Moore prior to their second fight in January, 1941. Shorty would defeat Moore to go 2-0 up in their series (*San Diego Tribune* January 31, 1941).

Rated Seventh

Shorty Hogue Signs to Box Burley Here

SHORTY HOGUE AND HIS BELT
He won the California title

Shorty Hogue shows off his California state championship belt (*Minneapolis Star*, December 29, 1941).

OLD TOM JONES AND HIS HOGUE TWINS
Don't ask which is Shorty! Who knows?

The twins with their manager, Tom Jones

The twins in action during an exhibition at Camp Grant.
Bill Goertz photograph, courtesy of Hans Ellund).

Joe Louis sees the sights at Fort Custer with the Hogue twins, middleweight oxers who appear next Friday night on a card at the Coliseum here. Both Shorty eft) and Big Boy (right) seem to express considerable zest as they entertain the top an in their profession.

The twins with Joe Louis during a visit to Fort Custer.

BURLEY BATTERS HOGUE INTO KAYO

Here's Charley Burley cutting down the taller and heavier Shorty Hogue before knocking out the young California middleweight in the tenth and final round of their fight at the Armory Friday night. The clever and sharpshooting Pittsburgh Negro stabbed and hooked Hogue dizzy with his rapier-like left hand and rocked him from head to heels with jolting rights.—(Morning Tribune Sportphoto.)

(Top to bottom) Shorty under attack from Charley Burley - Shorty goes down in the 10th round vs Burley.

'I'll Give Lester This Tonight'

The twins hamming it up for the press prior to Big Boy's fight with Kid Lester (September 19, 1943).

Shorty and Big Boy Hogue (Photo courtesy of Mike Silver).

ACKNOWLEDGEMENTS

As is usually the case, it took a good many people to assist in the research for (and the writing of) this book. Be it family histories, stories, press or magazine clippings, photographs, fact-checking or cups of tea — not to mention the endless patience (as I take far too long to do just about anything).

So, thank you to (in no particular order); the late Bob Dye, Lori (Dye) Grove, Hoby Hogue, the Plummers, Mike Silver, the late Gabrielle 'Hap' Navarro, Alister Scott Ottesen, Dan Cuoco (and my fellow members of the International Boxing Research Organisation), Doug Dickey, Chuck Hasson, Douglas Cavanaugh, Miles Ugakovich, Jerry Fitch, Cherry Diefenbach (Jacumba), Judith Merriott, Hans Eland (for the Bill Goertz photographs - Boekenpakhuis.co.nl), Clinton Jones (bluelotus.co.nz) for the artwork (p193 and p199), John Ochs for the editing and fine-tuning (and, by default the late J. Michael Kenyon for the same), also to my wife, Sandra, for putting up with me. Apologies to anyone I may have missed, it was not my intention to do so.

SOURCES

A number of newspaper resources were utilised for this book. Some quotes or information - particularly those relating to the Hogue twins' early boxing career - are taken from press clippings found in a Hogue family scrapbook. Often, said clippings did not contain a date or even a publication. Where possible I have tracked down the original source and have quoted applicable dates etc. However, some gaps still exist due to a lack of archived material relating to specific publications of the period.

All other citations include the publication, the original publication date and the page on which said citation appears in the book.

* * *

NEWSPAPERS

Arizona Republic: May 10, 1952 (p167), May 28, 1952 (p167), June 1, 1952 (p167-168)

Brawley Press: July 22, 1936 (p21), July 29, 1936 (p22), April 21, 1937 (p23)

Daily News-Miner (Fairbanks), May 10, 1957 (p158)

El Centro Morning Post: April 29, 1937 (p24), April 29, 1937 (p25), *December 1938(p43)*

Fresno Bee: Jan 20, 1940 (p81-82), December 21, 1940 (p96-97)

Hayward Review: March 9, 1943 (p146-147)

Hollywood Pic magazine: March, 1940 (p84)

Imperial Times: June 23, 1937 (p29), July 21, 1937 (p30)

Imperial Valley Press: (p30), September 23, 1938 (p38)

LA Examiner: (December 1, 1938) (p40),, December 19, 1938 (p45)

LA Times: December 1938 (p43), March 13, 1939 (p59), April 12, 1939 (p60-61), August 5, 1939 (p66), August 29, 1939 (p68-69), August 23, 1941(p111), July 22, 1942 (p130)

Minneapolis Daily Times: January 10, 1942 (p55), January 10, 1942 (p79), January 10, 1942 (p119), January 10, 1942 (p99)

Minneapolis Star: January 5, 1942, January 6, 1942, January 8, January 10, 1942 (p1), (p17), (p35), (p55), January 10, 1942 (p122)

Modesto Bee: December 9, 1939 (p73), October, 8, 1940 (p93-94), April 25, 1942 (p127), July 23, 1943 (p148)

Nevada State Journal June 8, 1940 (p86), September 13, 1942 (p134), July 23, 1943 (p148), May 17, 1944 (p151-152),(May 24, 1944) (p152)

Oakland Tribune, August 19, 1940 (p89-90), August 18, 1940 (p90), August 19, 1940 (p90), August 20, 1940 (p91), December 21, 1940 (p97), February 8, 1941(p106), March 8, 1941 (p106), September 19, 1942 (p135)

Reno Evening Gazette, October 25, 1940 (p94-95)

San Diego Evening Tribune, December 12, 1938 (p47), January 31, 1941 (p101-102)

San Diego Union, August 2, 1935, August 27, 1939, March 31 1939, March 10, 1939, February 20, 1939 (p50), June, 8 1939 (p64), August 15, 1939 (p67), July 13, 1939 (p65), December 30, 1939 (p75), February 15, 1940 (p82-83), *(p83),* August 28, 1940 (p88), March 15, 1941(p108), January 30, 1942 (p123), February 7, 1942 (p124), February 14, 1942 (p125), *April 25 1942(p127),* July 22, 1942 (p132), August 15, 1942 (p134), August 13, 1944 (p153), *San Diego Union-Tribune:* April 7, 1993 (p179), *San Diego Union* October 26, 1961, *San Diego Union-Tribune:* December 25, 1999.

San Francisco Chronicle August 20, 1940 (p91), December 20 1940 (96)

The Signal (Santa Clarita) *December 1, 1971 (p175)*

Sunday Gleaner, January 15, 1967 (p126)

Telegram Tribune (San Luis Obispo) March 9, 1943 (p139-140)

PERIODICALS

The Knockout: July 25, 1942 (p129-130)

The Referee, August 24, 1940 (p90-91), October 12, 1940 (p92-93)

THE RING April 1939 (p51 and p52), July 1939 (p62), August 1939 (p63), September 1939 (p63), December 1939 (p71), February 1940 (p74), March 1940 (p75), April 1940 (p81), March 1940 (p82), July 1940 (p85-86), September 1940 (87), November, 1940 (p92), July 1941(p109), October 1941 (p110-111), April 1942 (p122), May 1942 (p124), September 1942 (p128), October 1942 (p128-129), (October, 1942) (p130), October 1942 (p132), November 1942 (p133), December 1942 (p134-135), December 1942 (p135-136), December 1943 (p149-150), March 1943 (p151), May 1981 (p178-179).

BOOKS

Cantu, RC. (ed) *Boxing and Medicine.* Human Kinetics. 1995.

Jordan, Barry D. *Medical Aspects of Boxing.* CRC Press. 1993.

Moore, Archie. *The Archie Moore Story.* The Sportsman's Book Club. 1960

Moore, Archie and Pearl, Leonard. *Any Boy Can.* Prentice Hall. 1971.

Otty, Harry. *Charley Burley and the Black Murderers' Row.* Tora Book Publishing. 2010.

Toledo, Springs. *Murderers' Row: in search of boxing's greatest outcasts.* Tora Book Publishing. 2017.

WEBSITES

Boxrec.com; Newspaperarchives.com, Genealogybank.com; Ancestry.com; Family-search.com; Ibroresearch.com; Cyberboxingzone.com; Thesandiegoreader.com (November 2016 - 'Jacumba is Really Out There'.

FILM

64 Day Hero: A Boxer's Tale (1986). Gordon Williams (Writer), Franco Rossso (Director)

INTERVIEWS, CONVERSATIONS, COMMUNICATIONS

Bob Dye: Personal emails - 2008; Lori Dye (Grove): Personal emails - May-December, 2008; Archie Moore letters to Bob Dye and Richard Plummer (1993) courtesy of Lori Dye; Hogue twins scrapbook (amateur careers) courtesy of Lori Dye, Big Boy Hogue home movies courtesy of Hoby Hogue. Press clippings of Burley vs Shorty Hogue from scrapbook of Charley Burley, courtesy of the late Julia Burley. Gabrielle 'Hap' Navarro: Personal emails (Jan and Feb) 2010.

Shorty Hogue Naval Service Records (79pp) obtained from National Personnel Records Centre, St. Louis, Missouri, September 27, 2010.

INDEX

Freeman, Tommy 108

Freitas, Johnny 71

Fresno Bee 74, 82, 92, 97, 106, 134

G

Garland, Tommy 60-62, 69-71

Garrison, Jimmy72, 85

Gavras, Joe 52

Georgino, Carmen 64

Gillespie, Jack 131

Gonzales, Joe (21) Art 21, 23, 37, 43, 44

Gorman, Britt 7, 55, 122

Graziano, Rocky 126

Grey, Nan 49

Gugler, William 42

H

Hagler, Marvelous Marvin 136-37

Haliman, Lester 157

Harris, Ulysses 'Uley' 28, 29, 63

Harrison, Roy 42

Hendrickson, Joe 5, 17, 35,122

Henneberry, Fred 103, 109

Hernandez, Babe 71

Higgins, Frank, C. 57

Hogue, Betty 10

Hogue, B. H. (Duge) 10, 13, 14

Hogue, Jessie, 10

Hogue, Jewell 10, 12

Hogue, Jimmie 32, 169, 170

Hogue, Lon (Alonzo) 10, 11, 19

Hogue, Nip 10, 13, 14, 31, 147, 159

Hogue, Pearl 10, 11

Harry Otty was born and raised in Liverpool, England.

He graduated from Liverpool John Moore University with a Bachelor of Science and from Manchester University with a Bachelor of Arts.

He is a life-long boxing fan whose other passion (besides researching boxing history) is coaching. He has produced numerous national and international champions in the UK and in New Zealand, where he currently lives with his wife and children.

His first book - *Charley Burley and the Black Murderers' Row*, Tora Book Publishing (ISBN 978-0-9543924-2-0) is available from Amazon.com and other book-sellers.

He can be contacted via his website - charleyburley.com

www.ingramcontent.com/pod-product-compliance
Lightning Source LLC
Chambersburg PA
CBHW021957090426
42811CB00001B/67